The Second

FRANK MUIR GOES INTO...

FRANK MUIR AND SIMON BRETT

Star

A STAR BOOK
published by
The Paperback Division of
W. H. Allen & Co. Ltd

A Star Book
Published in 1980
by the Paperback Division of W. H. Allen & Co. Ltd
A Howard and Wyndham Company
44 Hill Street, London W1X 8LB

First published in Great Britain by Robson Books Ltd., 1979

Copyright © 1979 Frank Muir and Simon Brett

ISBN 0 352 30650 5

Designed by Harold King

Photos of Frank Muir by Gemma Levine

Picture research Harold King, Lynda Poley.

Picture sources:
The Fotomas Library, Topham, Punch
and grateful thanks to the London Library.

Permission to use extracts from the following copyright material is gratefully acknowledged: *This England* by Michael Bateman (Statesman and Nation Publishing Co.); *Funny Ha Ha and Funny Peculiar* and *Funny Amusing and Funny Amazing* by Denys Parsons (Pan Books); 'Godolphin Horne' and 'Hildebrand' by Hilaire Belloc from his *Cautionary Verses* (A. D. Peters); G. K. Chesterton verse from his *Ballads of an Anti-Puritan* (A. P. Watt & Son); Walter de la Mare verse from *The Complete Poems of Walter de la Mare* (Literary Trustees of Walter de la Mare and the Society of Authors as their representative.

Printed in Great Britain
by W & J Mackay Limited, Chatham

CONTENTS

PREFACE

Simon Brett and I have mixed views about Prefaces. At best, as in Bernard Shaw's Prefaces to his plays, they are a superb prelude to the main event. At worst they are an intolerable nuisance which stops you getting *to* the main event, like a protracted Wedding Breakfast.

There is nothing really to be said in a Preface to this book. The world knows from the first book that it is a compilation of the humour which certain subjects attract. That it has affiliations to the radio programme of the same name. That it contains the new wonder ingredient — GLEE.

Our favourite Preface in all literature comes from a little-known novel by Amanda McKittrick Ros, who wrote two and a half astonishing novels, a book or two of incredible poems — all well worth searching for — before dying in 1939. Mrs Ros was a vast Irish lady, married to the station-master of the tiny port of Larne in Northern Ireland. She was well aware that she was one of the greatest writers the world had ever known and had not one vestige of a trace of even a hint of a sense of humour. I can best describe her as a prose McGonagall. This is the Preface to her second novel, *Delina Delaney*. How superbly she sums it all up!

Preface

No matter how strong or weak the attempt to lay before this world of literary differences a subject for perusal, its inhabitants (whose patronage is worthy of every consideration) hunger very often for what is termed a Preface. I, for one, have a natural dislike for writing a Preface to any of my works, being so trivial in themselves as not to warrant the most trivial word of introduction.

Suffice it to say that, although I treat with dislike the thought of augmenting my fragile works with more fragile words, jumbled into the form of a Preface, yet, I must confess, duty has grooved a means at last to tamper with my resolution. Therefore, my readers, if not granted the express privilege of perusing a Preface to this work, will please remain satisfied, for the time being, with the matter contained in the first few pages of this book, and regard it as one which, if it fail to be placed on the shelf of Prefaces, won't fail to elicit, at least, from the lips of those who read it, a word of approval.

Sincerely thine,

AMANDA M. ROS

OPTIMISM

After a long course of psychiatric treatment the patient was cured. 'Well,' said the psychiatrist, 'your life's in front of you now. What are you going to do with it?

'Well,' said the patient, 'I've got high academic qualifications, so I can really take my pick of jobs. I might try the Law, Politics, Advertising, Public Relations, Management, Broadcasting, Writing maybe. On the other hand I might go back to being a teapot.'

Did you hear about the man who wanted to cross a carrier-pigeon with a woodpecker to get a bird that would knock on the door before delivering a message?

Paddy and Seamus were walking through the woods when they saw a sign up saying, 'Tree Fellers Wanted'. 'Ah, isn't that a shame,' said Paddy. 'If only we had Michael with us, we might get the jobs.'

'I'm breeding a new animal. Have great hopes for it.'
   'What is it?'
   'It's half parrot and half tiger.'
   'Is it a good talker?'
   'It doesn't actually say much. But when it does, YOU LISTEN.'

An Aberdeen couple were shipwrecked on a desert island. After a week their clothes were torn to shreds, their provisions had run out and they were exhausted. 'Oh Jock,' said the wife, 'things just couldn't be worse.'

'They could that,' said Jock. 'We might have bought return tickets.'

A cavalry officer was bawling out a young recruit on a horse. 'Trooper Botting, you've only got one spur on.'

'I know that, sir,' replied Trooper Botting, 'but I reckon if I get one side of the horse to go, the other will probably go as well.'

An Irishman was boasting about how he kept his money in a sock under his bed. 'But that's daft,' said his friend. 'You're losing interest that way.'

'I am not,' came the dignified reply. 'Sure and I put a bit aside for that too.'

'Look at that girl walking along the promenade. What's she doing?'

'She's looking for her boyfriend.'

'Oh, what's his name?'

'She doesn't know yet.'

'Our new football team is sensational — no losses, no draws, no goals scored against them.'

'How many matches have they played?'

'First one's Sunday.'

A secretary came into her office one morning at half past ten and found her boss glowering at her empty chair. 'Oh come on, Mr Brown,' she said winningly, 'this is the earliest I've been late this week.'

'Of course we must face facts.
It's going to mean waiting'

Optimism in humour tends to be rather short-lived and I'm afraid the funny part usually occurs when a man's optimism is shown to be ill-founded. There are many comic characters based on the conflict between their own blind conviction that things will work and the inexorable law of nature that they won't. Don Quixote is a good early example and most slapstick gains strength from the juxtaposition of confidence and incompetence. But optimism is a desirable human quality. Alexander Pope:

Hope springs eternal in the human breast;
Man never is, but always to be blessed.

But optimism without fulfilment is not enough. Francis Bacon:

Hope is a good breakfast, but it is a bad supper.

(Come to think of it, Bacon is a good breakfast.)

An optimist, almost by definition, needs a degree of blindness about the future. Kin Hubbard:

An optimist is a fellow who believes what's going to be
will be postponed.

Optimism often inspires cynicism in those who lack it. Here's an epigram by Samuel Butler (the seventeenth-century one):

Far greater numbers have been lost by hopes,
Than all the magazines of daggers, ropes,
And other ammunitions of despair,
Were ever able to dispatch, by fear.

11

Ambrose Bierce, in his *Devil's Dictionary*, provided a predictably cynical definition:

> OPTIMISM, n. The doctrine, or belief, that everything is beautiful, including what is ugly, everything good, especially the bad, and everything right that is wrong. It is held with greatest tenacity by those most accumstomed to the mischance of falling into adversity, and is most acceptably expounded with the grin that apes smile. Being a blind faith, it is inaccessible to the light of disproof — an intellectual disorder, yielding to no treatment but death. It is hereditary, but fortunately not contagious.

In these cynical times optimism is unfashionable and even genuine optimists may feel obliged to hide their optimism behind a mask of pessimism. Perhaps a few more definitions will make it easier to spot the difference between the two. First, here's one from James Branch Cabell:

> The optimist proclaims that we live in the best of all possible worlds; and the pessimist fears this is true.

From McLandburgh Wilson:

> 'Twixt optimist and pessimist
> The difference is droll —
> The optimist sees the doughnut,
> The pessimist the hole.

The Americans are rather keen on that sort of paradox. Here's another from a one-time United States Senator, Chauncey Depew:

> A pessimist thinks all women are bad; an optimist hopes they are.

And, while we're talking about women, an observation from Ring Lardner:

> An optimist is a girl who mistakes a bulge for a curve.

It's important for an optimist, whatever disaster faces him, to look on the bright side. It's part of all those old clichés about whether a glass is half-full or half-empty, or which alternative you take from the options in this anonymous poem:

> **Two men looked out through prison bars —**
> **One saw mud; the other stars.**

But whatever happens, you have to make the best of it. Walter Winchell:

> **An optimist is a man who is treed by a lion, but enjoys**
> **the scenery.**

Criminals are rather good at this sort of optimism. They seem to retain the cheerful hope that their unlikeliest stories will be believed in court. Let's look at some examples from the press. First, a report in *The Sutton Times:*

> **When asked why he was carrying a heavy iron gate hinge**
> **early in the morning at the premises of a Croydon firm,**
> **he was alleged to have replied, 'I was going to make a**
> **bird-cage.'**

From the *Bristol Evening Post:*

> **A Southmead man, found with a screwdriver and a pair**
> **of wirecutters in Canford Park last night, was said to**
> **have told police he used them to adjust his artificial leg.**

And the *Herts and Essex Observer:*

> **When the Sergeant was fined £2 for travelling on the**
> **railway without paying his fare, he produced a warrant**
> **which had already been used for a previous journey. A**
> **railway official said that when asked to explain previous**
> **clip marks on the warrant, defendant said, 'Moths.'**

And if you believe that, you'll believe anything.

But there are more serious matters in modern life, which require a hopeful outlook to maintain one's sanity. The proliferation and development of new weapons tax our resources of optimism considerably. It's a great comfort that the British stiff upper lip still retains its starch. Here's a report from *Illustrated Magazine:*

'There is a simple answer to the atomic bomb,' says dapper, quiet-voiced Brigadier A. M. Toye, VC, MC. 'It is that no weapon has ever been invented for which the answer does not exist.'

'It's going to make war impossible'

What a comfort that is. And while we're on the subject of nuclear weapons, let's read a little more reassurance from the *Bath and Wilts Chronicle*:

> 'Once a nuclear bomb has dropped in your area it is unlikely that there will ever be another one in the district,' says Dr. G. D. Kersley... Writing in this week's *British Medical Journal*, he suggests that this is one 'reassuring' point which might be told the public to reduce panic during a nuclear war.

And a useful tip from the *Brighton Evening Argus:*

> 'If you want to safeguard your children against atomic radiation and fall-out, take them to Brighton's sea-front cliffs and let them eat chalk.' This was a physicist's advice to 250 people in Brighton last night.

And, if they survive that, I should think they'd take a nuclear attack in their stride. You see, for every situation somebody comes up with a cure or a remedy. That's a source of comfort. Whatever new disasters are threatened, there's always an inventor tucked away somewhere working on an antidote.

Invention is a calling which requires a great deal of optimism, belief that your idea will work, and is worth pursuing anyway. There must be a wonderful sense of achievement when the prototype is finally made. From the *News Chronicle*:

> **'I am glad to be able to tell the House,' Mr Bellinger said, 'that the Army has been experimenting with an unpolishable button.'**

I thought they all were. When you're inventing something you have to be very careful and make sure that your product is tested in all the conditions which it is likely to encounter in use. A report from the *Southport Guardian*:

> **He had sold dozens of pairs of these swimming trunks made of a new plastic material before someone discovered it was soluble in water.**

There are always hundreds of people around with good ideas. Here's a useful suggestion from a letter published in the *Daily Mirror:*

> **Dandruff may be contacted by resting the head against infected upholstery in railway carriages. I suggest, therefore, that railway carriages should be boiled for twenty minutes at each station or halt.**

The belief that that idea would be accepted must have involved optimism of a very high order. Or perhaps something else. Havelock Ellis:

> **The place where optimism most flourishes is the lunatic asylum.**

The mad inventor is a popular figure in fiction, but in most cases inventors are guilty of nothing worse than naiveté. Their ideas seem so good to them that they get blinded to the claims of reality. Here's an idea from the *Daily Telegraph* in the late 'sixties:

> **Lord Alastair Graham, St Edmundsbury and Ipswich, suggested that the Church should send up a sputnik into outer space with a bishop inside it, which would draw the attention of millions towards God.**

If the hopes of optimists were fulfilled, that idea would be a very good one (except that, if the hopes of optimists were fully fulfilled, it wouldn't be necessary to draw the attention of millions towards God).

But the optimist has to believe he lives in an ideal world. As Voltaire says in *Candide* (not without irony):

> **All is for the best in this best of all possible worlds.**

This comforting philosophy is elaborated in Alexander Pope's *Essay on Man* (and he really believed it):

> **All nature is but art, unknown to thee,**
> **All chance, direction which thou canst not see;**
> **All discord, harmony not understood;**
> **All partial evil, universal good;**
> **And, spite of pride, in erring reason's spite,**
> **One truth is clear, Whatever is, is right.**

That view may have changed slightly since the Augustan Age. Here's a report from the *Daily Express*:

> **In yesterday's *Daily Express*, Mr Gallacher, Communist MP for West Fife, was wrongly reported as saying that the British Empire got nearer to our dream of a perfect world than anything else that existed.**

A healthier attitude is expressed in this post-war letter published in the *News Chronicle*:

> **Our people in the past have built empires, invented wonders, withstood blitzes and won wars on the good, plain cooking of the Englishwoman. I am confident they will win the peace on the same stuff.**

That's the message — look on the bright side, whatever happens. Every cloud has a silver wedding. All's for the best, in spite of disasters. Here's an anonymous poem, which looks on the bright side:

> **I have lost my mistress, horse and wife,**
> **And when I think of human life,**
> **Cry mercy 'twas no worse,**
> **My mistress sickly, poor and old,**
> **My wife damn'd ugly and a scold —**
> **I am sorry for my horse.**

You see, it's an ill wind. Things are never as bad as they seem. And if you believe in something, as every film musical will tell you, you cannot fail. The human spirit is indomitable. A little verse from Henry Luttrell:

> **O death, thy certainty is such,**
> **And thou'rt a thing so fearful,**
> **That, musing, I have wonder'd much**
> **How men were ever cheerful.**

But men do remain cheerful. There are examples of optimism everywhere. You see them in the press daily — small ads from young hopefuls who really think someone will want to buy their clapped-out old car or that someone will sell them a house at a price that they can afford. You have to be optimistic when you're trying to find accommodation. Here's an advertisement from the magazine *Our Dogs*:

Business lady and gentleman would like to rent ground-floor rooms or flat in North London in order to breed a litter of Wire Fox-terriers, very careful tenants, no children.

Another from the *Wallasey Times*:

Unfurnished self-contained flat, 2 bedrooms, urgently required at moderate rent by Customs Officer and wife expecting quiet baby.

They'd be lucky. So would the hopeful parents who put this advertisement in the *Manchester Evening News*:

Will the parents of the boy who gave a little boy an apple in exchange for his tricycle outside the Sale Lido on Friday between six and seven, kindly return it at once?

Yes, you have to be optimistic, right to the end. For a close to the chapter, let's have the last words of Lord Palmerston:

'Die, my dear Doctor? That's the last thing I shall do!'

All Deformities permanently cured by Dr. J. P. MANN,
No. 133 West 41st St., New York   Send for Circular.

PESSIMISM

'I don't know which irritates me more—pessimists or non-conformists'

Two old friends met in the street. 'Hello, Walter, long time no see. How are you?'

'Oh, terrible, Nigel, terrible. Everything's going wrong. My wife's gone off with another man, my son's in prison and the house has burnt down.'

'Oh dear 'oh dear 'oh dear. And what are you doing at the moment?'

'Selling lucky charms.'

'Here, shopkeeper, this broom you sold me is hopeless.'

'Why?'

'Well, the head's fallen off four times and now the handle's come out.'

Two men meet in the pub. 'I say, Lionel,' says one of them, 'your're looking pretty tired. What's up?'

'Oh, it's the wife, Cecil. Always fears the worst and the result is I don't get any sleep. You see, every time she hears a noise in the night she makes me go down to see if we've got burglars.'

'Oh, you must tell her, Lionel, that's nonsense. Apart from anything else, burglars are very quiet people. If there were any in your house, they wouldn't make any noise.'

'I know, Cecil. I told her that. Now I have to keep getting up because she can't hear anything.'

'Doctor, doctor, my son's just swallowed seventeen and a half pence.'

'How is he?'

'No change yet.'

'Doctor, doctor, how am I?'

'Well, I...er...'

'I mean, doctor, can I sit up in bed and read?'

'Yes, but don't start any serials.'

An insurance salesman was trying to persuade a young wife to take out a policy on her husband's life and working round to the subject rather gingerly. She didn't seem to understand, so he tried a more direct approach. 'Look at it this way. If your husband died tomorrow, what would you get?'

'Oh,' she said, 'probably a budgie.

A woman going into a posh wedding was stopped at the church door by an usher. 'Excuse me, are you a friend of the groom?'

'No,' she replied, 'I'm the bride's mother.'

A young golfer found his ball deeply embedded in a bunker. 'Which club do you think I should use, caddie?'

The caddie looked him straight in the eyes. 'The way you play,' he replied, 'it doesn't matter.'

Cohen noticed that his friend Levy was looking unhappy. 'Is something worrying you?' he asked.

'Listen,' said Levy, 'I have so many worries that, if something happens today, I won't have time to worry about it for another month.'

'Precisely the same as they said about poor Frederic, my dear, and he scarcely lasted the week'

Pessimism is in everyone's nature at times. Fortunately in most of us it's balanced by moods of optimism, but pessimism can sometimes be very funny. There are many comedians whose stock-in-trade is a gloomy outlook on life. For an audience it can be extremely amusing to hear someone cataloguing the disasters which are likely to befall him. Pessimism is, as we all know, fearing — and indeed expecting — the worst. For some closer definitions let's turn first to George Bernard Shaw:

Do you know what a pessimist is? A man who thinks everybody as nasty as himself and hates himself for it.

Here's another from Elbert Hubbard:

A pessimist is one who has been intimately acquainted with an optimist.

Yes, life with an eternally cheerful Pollyanna must be very wearing. But I don't know that the company of pessimists is any better. Jean Rostand:

My pessimism goes to the point of suspecting the sincerity of the pessimists.

Pessimism is frowned on by those who uphold the old values that made this country great. G. K. Chesterton:

Pessimism — a thing unfit for a white man.

But it does, nonetheless, have its pleasures. Arnold Bennett:

Pessimism, when you get used to it, is just as agreeable as optimism.

In fact, it's possible to have an utterly gloomy outlook on life and still remain quite jolly about it. Here's some morbid self-indulgence from John H. Frere:

Despair in vain sits brooding over the putrid eggs of hope.

Gustave Flaubert had a similar outlook:

> **While still very young I had a complete presentiment of life. It was like a nauseating kitchen smell that pours through a ventilator: you don't have to eat the food cooked in such a place to know that it would make you vomit.**

Cheery soul. Let's have more gloom from Ben Jonson:

> **What a deal of cold business doth a man mis-spend the better part of life in! in scattering compliments, tendring visits, gathering and venting news, following Feasts and Playes, making a little winter-love in a darke corner.**

Somehow that sort of pessimism, particularly when it's expressed in such beautiful language, doesn't have much effect. The knowledge that life is futile need not stop you enjoying it. Of course some people have more cause than others for misery because of their material circumstances. Here's an extract from the introduction to a catalogue of paintings:

> **Material misfortune seemed to dog him. He was half killed in an accident to the ambulance he served; his house was destroyed in the blitz and all his unsold paintings with it: he was employed by the BBC.**

Given that sort of suffering, it is not surprising that some people get irretrievably pessimistic and want to end it all. When Benjamin Franklin was ill, a well-wisher came and said: 'I hope you will get better.' To which Franklin replied: 'I hope not.'

Here's a similarly pessimistic verse by Thomas Hardy:

> **EPITAPH ON A PESSIMIST**
> **I'm Smith of Stoke, aged sixty-odd,**
> ** I've lived without a dame**
> **From youth-time on: and would to God**
> ** My dad had done the same.**

But even for people as gloomy as that, there are compensations. A little fable from Ambrose Bierce:

> A pessimist applied to God for relief.
>
> 'Ah, you wish me to restore your hope and cheerfulness,' said God.
>
> 'No,' replied the petitioner, 'I wish you to create something that would justify them.'
>
> 'The world is all created,' said God, 'but you have overlooked something — the mortality of the optimist.'

However, a pessimist is by his nature unable to keep seeing the bright side for very long. And when life seems totally without hope, people do resort to desperate measures. Here's a report from the old *Manchester Guardian:*

> It was alleged at Caerphilly yesterday that when a young collier, who was lying across a railway track on Sunday night with the intention of committing suicide, was told by a porter that there would be no train on that line until yesterday morning, nine hours later, he replied, 'I'll wait till then.'

Suicide is an extreme form of pessimism, but the feeling is always around in lesser ways. Sometimes its presence is not deliberate, just an unwritten admission that the worst will probably happen. This is particularly true on public notices and advertisements. First, here's one from a café:

Customers who consider our waitresses uncivil should see the manager.

An advertisement from a Rhodesian newspaper:

We can safely say that there is no repair job necessary on a car that cannot be executed more efficiently than by us.

Or one from the *Los Angeles Times:*

FOOT TROUBLES RELIEVED
Custom-made arches designed and made for your particular discomfort.

That sort of thing can be very discouraging to potential customers. But there are other ways of bringing people down. Here's a report from the *Sunday Express:*

Margate Corporation has a new slogan: 'There's life in the Margate air'. It is being sent to all parts of the country on envelopes containing reminders that cemetery fees for the year are due.

That could be interpreted as prudent future planning. Even if you are not a total pessimist, it pays to look ahead. From the old *News Chronicle:*

Parishioners at Beeston Regis (Norfolk) are making plans for the year 2192. Calculating that the sea will menace their Parish Church about that time, they are asking the Church Council to open a fund which will enable it to be removed further inland.

News from the *Daily Mirror:*

Among the town's new proposed by-laws is one that imposes a fine of up to £2 on any trolley-bus passenger who 'throws money to be scrambled for by any person on

the road or footway'. An official said, 'There is no particular reason for the by-law. It's just a safety precaution.'

Mind you, if you look even further ahead, it can land you in trouble. Here's a report from a wartime *Daily Sketch*:

Mr H. Clarke, prosecuting, said Bradshaw returned his enrolment notice with the message: 'I object to fire-watching as it appears to me to be an attempt to prevent the fulfilment of the Scripture which says that the world will be destroyed by fire.'

Even if your view of life isn't quite that apocalyptic, it can still be a depressing business when reduced to its bare essentials. Here's a bleak poem by the nineteenth-century writer, Ben King, entitled *The Pessimist:*

Nothing to do but work,
Nothing to eat but food,
Nothing to wear but clothes
To keep one from going nude.

Nothing to breathe but air
Quick as a flash 'tis gone;
Nowhere to fall but off,
Nowhere to stand but on.

Nothing to comb but hair,
Nowhere to sleep but in bed,
Nothing to weep but tears,
Nothing to bury but dead.

Nothing to sing but songs,
Ah, well, alas! alack!
Nowhere to go but out,
Nowhere to come but back.

After reading something like that, you could be tempted to wonder whether it's all worthwhile. Ambrose Bierce:

Before undergoing a surgical operation — arrange your temporal affairs; you may live.

The argument for pessimism runs that it's not a gloomy view of life, just an acceptance of reality, an ability to face the facts. Sometimes to accept the worst is the only logical solution, as in this report from the *Evening Standard:*

> **The vicar thinks it is impossible for his parishioners —
> most are boarding-house keepers — to keep all the Ten
> Commandments, so he reduced them to nine for his
> services.**

Which one? *Which one?* You never find out the interesting bits.

Another example of realistic pessimism from the Reverend Sydney Smith:

> **I am just going to pray for you at St Paul's, but with no
> very lively hope of success.**

Some people live all their lives in anticipation of disaster, while others need an actual disaster to make them aware of the dangers that surround them. Here's a letter published in the old *Manchester Guardian:*

> **The village of Stone in Buckinghamshire, which
> straddles the main Aylesbury-Oxford road, recently
> asked for a speed limit. The application was turned
> down on the grounds that there had not been enough
> accidents there yet.**

In case that idea has depressed you, I'll conclude with a thought from James Hagerty, which sums up everything there is left to say about pessimism:

> **One day I sat thinking, almost in despair; a hand fell on
> my shoulder and a voice said reassuringly, 'Cheer up,
> things could be worse.' So I cheered up, and sure enough
> — things got worse.**

NOSTALGIA

'Have you noticed how up-to-date the nostalgia's beginning to look'

Two old men were sitting in the park and they saw a pretty girl walk past. 'You know,' says one to the other, 'you remember that stuff they used to put in our tea during the Boer War, to keep our minds off it...?

'Yes.'

'Well, I think mine's beginning to work.'

An old woman's talking to her husband sentimentally about their courtship. 'Ah, do you remember how you used to nibble my ear?'

'Yes.'

'You never do it nowadays.'

'No. Well, by the time I've found my teeth, the urge has gone.'

An old soldier was telling a rather bored young man about his military ancestry. 'Do you know, my great-grandfather fought with Wellington in 1810, my grandfather fought with Redvers Buller in 1870, my father fought with Kitchener in 1916, and I fought with Monty in 1942.'

'Oh dear,' the young man drawled, 'your family doesn't seem to have been able to get along with anyone.'

They were good days when I was a boy. We were poor, mind. My mother used to send me down to the butcher's every Monday to buy a sheep's head. And I had to ask him to leave the eyes in, so that it would see us through the week.

Two old blokes met in a gentlemen's club in London. 'Excuse me,' said one, 'is your name Ponsonby-Smythe?'

The other fellow took a large leather diary out of his pocket, flicked through the pages and, after a pause, replied, 'Yes.'

'Were you in India before the war?'

Again he consulted the diary. 'Yes.'

'Poona in '28?'

Once more the pages of the dairy were flicked through. 'Yes.'

'Did you know a Lady Carruthers-Pyke?'

A longer consultation with the diary was required before he replied, 'Yes.'

'Did you sleep with her?'

This question required even more research in the diary. But eventually, 'Yes.'

At this the first gentleman stamped his foot and shouted, 'Well, I'm Lord Carruthers-Pyke and I don't like it!'

The second gentleman flicked through his diary for another reference, found it and said, 'Neither did I.'

An old married couple were lying in bed and the wife said wistfully, 'Do you remember, when we were first married and got into bed, you hardly gave me time to get my stockings off.'

'Ah,' sighed the old man, 'now you'd have time to knit yourself a pair.'

Two former members of the diplomatic service meet in London. 'I say, do you remember that fellow Winthrop we knew out in Rio? Great chap he was.'

'Winthrop? Oh, I remember, yes. What's he up to these days?'

'Last thing I heard he had gone completely off his rocker and gone off into the jungle to live with a monkey.'

'Good Lord. Fancy that. Well, my oh my, things have changed. Was it a male monkey or a female monkey?'

'Oh, female. There's nothing funny about Winthrop.'

I used to be very keen on football when I was young. Mind you, it was a different game in those days. Different sense of values. I once went to the local stadium, gave a shilling and asked for two and the man on the gate said, 'Half-backs or forwards?'

Two old soldiers were arguing over the respective merits of their regiments. 'Oh, ours was the best of the lot, Lionel.'

'Not as good as ours, Rollo old man. We were the best drill squad in the world in those days. When we presented arms, all you could hear was "Slap-2-3-Slap-2-3-Slap". As one man.'

'Oh, our lot was better than that, Lionel. When we presented arms, all you could hear was "Slap-2-3-Slap-2-3-Slap-2-3-Jingle".'

'Jingle? What was the jingle?'

'Medals.'

Nostalgia is one of those many words in the English language whose popular meaning is different from its real meaning. Originally it meant home-sickness, but increasingly it has come to be used to describe a more general feeling of regret for familiar things and, particularly, regret for the past.

Some people don't think the past has much more to recommend it than the present. Here's Ambrose Bierce's definition:

PAST, n. That part of Eternity with some small fraction of which we have a slight and regrettable acquaintance.

But a more general view is that the past had a lot going for it, at least by comparison with what's going on now. Shakespeare encapsulated the thought in *Henry IV Part 2*:

Past and to come seems best; things present, worst.

That's always much of the appeal of looking back; it takes your mind off the reality that faces you; it's sheer escapism. And the worse the present becomes, the more attractive are former times.

Nowadays the nostalgia cycle is getting shorter and shorter. Plays and films are being produced about the 'fifties and even the 'sixties, and people are buying the bric-à-brac of ten years ago at vastly inflated prices. Nostalgia is big business, particularly in entertainment. Soon the cycle will speed up so much that some smart operator will write a modern show that's nostalgic as soon as it's written.

The nostalgia boom is perhaps a sad comment on the current state of the world. It's in times of uncertainty that people look back with such intensity to the apparently more fixed standards of an earlier time. Things must have been better then. Lord Byron:

The good old times — all times, when old, are good — are gone.

But, in spite of the gloom cast by today's newspapers, it's not just that things are particularly bad at the moment. Mankind always has looked back. Every civilisation has its epic poems and stories recounting the deeds of heroes long dead, and shares the feeling that the present can only produce pale imitations of former glories. Some people always live in the past. Here's a little poem by Walter de la Mare:

Do diddle di do,
Poor Jim Jay
Got stuck fast
In yesterday.

And there's a lovely comment on the British upper middle classes in John Osborne's *Look Back in Anger:*

They spend their time mostly looking forward to the past.

Enthusiastic Lady (at Musical At Home). 'Do you remember what this tune is out of, Doctor? Used to be all the rage when we were in our 'teens. Tum—tum—tum—tum—tum—tum—tum—tum?'
Eminent Dyspepsia Specialist. 'The words are familiar.'

There's a strong conviction that everything was more reliable in the past, and you need reliability in times of trouble. Here's a report from a wartime edition of *The Observer*:

> **There is one trade which continues to flourish through bad times: that is the corsetry trade. The greater the difficulties ahead, the more women feel that they should fortify themselves with the support not of the light elastic belts of peacetime, but with corsets that really control the figure. In Marshall and Snelgrove's department, for instance, the honest corset of former times has come back.**

The trouble with hindsight is that it tends to be inaccurate. The philosopher Locke described man's memory as a distorting glass and I am afraid that that glass is often rose-tinted. Not everyone wants total recall, anyway. Max Beerbohm saw it as a rather ordinary accomplishment:

> **To give an accurate and exhaustive account of that period would need a far less brilliant pen than mine.**

There's always something rather poignant about nostalgia. Half of its attraction lies in a sort of morbid wallowing in sadness, regret for the good times, even if they didn't seem that good while they were happening. In the words of François Villon:

> **Où sont les neiges d'antan?**

(Somehow that quotation has to be in French. The very sound of the words seems to carry regret. An English translation, like 'Where are the snows of yesteryear?', seems pale by comparison.)

Let's have a little more sentimentality, from Oliver Goldsmith:

> **O Memory! thou fond deceiver,**
> **Still importunate and vain,**
> **To former joys recurring ever,**
> **And turning all the past to pain.**

The past seems to bring out morbidity from poets. Here's more in similar vein from Alfred, Lord Tennyson:

Time driveth onward fast,
And in a little time our lips are dumb.
Let us alone. What is it that will last?
All things are taken from us, and become
Portions and parcels of the dreadful Past.

All of which brings to mind that famous philosophical remark of some anonymous graffiti artist:

Nostalgia isn't what it used to be.

Perhaps it's analysing the past that makes one low-spirited about it. Here's some homely wisdom reported in *The Morpeth Herald:*

Alderman G. Duddridge said it was no use holding a post mortem on something that was dead.

No, it's probably better just to look back on the rosy myths of childhood and remember how things might well have been. Lord Byron:

Ah, happy years! Once more who would not be a boy?

(I suppose the answer to that is: Most girls.) Here's a similar sentiment from Thomas Hood:

> Oh, when I was a tiny boy
> My days and nights were full of joy,
> My mates were blithe and kind! —
> No wonder that I sometimes sigh
> And dash the tear-drop from my eye
> To cast a look behind...
>
> Oh, for the lessons learned by heart!
> Ay, though the very birch's smart
> Should mark those hours again:
> I'd 'kiss the rod' and be resign'd
> Beneath the stroke, and even find
> Some sugar in the cane.

What he's saying, through that rather tortuous final image, is the old cliché that schooldays are supposed to be the happiest days of one's life. And, as with so many subjects for nostalgia, no one else's school experiences are quite as real as one's own. In retrospect, your own teachers were stricter, bullies crueller, athletes faster; no one else quite matches up. Here's Samuel Pepys on the subject:

> **Feb. 4th 1662. To Paul's Schoole, it being Opposition Day there. I heard some of their speeches, and they were just as schoolboys used to be, of the seven liberal sciences; but I think not as good as ours were in our time... Went up to see the head forms posed in Latin, Greek and Hebrew; but I think they did not answer in any so well as we did.**

The trouble is that one's school memories, like everything else, become very isolated, because there is so much change in simple things like the language of education. Many parents have found that, when they come to discuss school affairs with their children, there is an almost total lack of communication because of new terminology. And any parent who really wants to confuse himself should try helping his offspring with his mathematics homework, if the child has been taught on the new system of mathematics!

The constant changes of language make all memories difficult to share with the young. Here's a report from the *Daily Mail:*

> **Mr C. Adams, Chairman of Walberswick, Suffolk, Parish Council, called a tittertorter a butterwats when he was a boy. 'I suppose most people call it a see-saw now,' he told the Council yesterday.**

As one gets older, one is supposed to put away childish things, be they tittertorters or butterwats. Age is supposed to be a time of wisdom and reflection. Here's an adage from H. J. Byron:

> **The gardener's rule applies to youth and age:**
> **When young 'sow wild oats', but when old, grow sage.**

Not everyone views the past with respect, and some aren't afraid to speak ill of the dead. Here's a little nineteenth-century rhyme by Walter Savage Landor (which may possibly explain how he got his middle name):

> **George the First was always reckon'd**
> **Vile — but viler George the Second;**
> **And what mortal ever heard**
> **Any good of George the Third?**
> **When from earth the Fourth descended,**
> **God be praised, the Georges ended.**

(History has of course updated that since and produced a couple more Georges for television companies to make series about.)

The dead exercise a strong fascination for the living. What were they really like when they were alive? And that fascination is as strong when one is talking about ordinary people as when one is about kings. That's why it's so interesting to read what is written on tombstones — sometimes an epitaph can reveal a little flash of character and open like a casement on to a former age. Here's one from Oxfordshire:

Here lies Stephen Rumbold
He lived to the age of a hundred and one,
Sanguine and strong.
A hundred to one you don't live so long.

From Aberdeen:

Here lie the bones of Elizabeth Charlotte,
Born a virgin, died a harlot.
She was aye a virgin at seventeen,
A remarkable thing in Aberdeen.

And another from North of the Border:

Here lies my gude and gracious Auntie
Whom death has packed in his portmanty.

And, finally, the epitaph of Martin Elginbrod:

Here lie I, Martin Elginbrod.
Hae mercy on my soul, Lord God;
As I would do, were I Lord God,
And ye were Martin Elginbrod.

The trouble with epitaphs, like memoirs and, in fact, all historical writing, is that they can lie. Very few people get the chance of carving their own epitaphs; usually they have to rely on someone else. And it is difficult to be accurate about the past. Finley Peter Dunne:

What's fame after all? 'Tis apt to be what someone
writes on your tombstone.

The dead have little control over their reputations. Those who hope for lasting notoriety may well be quickly forgotten and those who only seek decent obscurity may not achieve it. But privacy should be everyone's right. Here's a plea for it in an anonymous epitaph, an English version of the Greek of Paulos:

Reader, pass on, nor idly waste your time,
In bad biography, or bitter rhyme;
What I am, this cumbrous clay ensures,
And what I was is no affair of yours.

But in spite of such deterrents, the urge to delve back into the past remains. People like memories, and where memory doesn't come up with the goods, very few people seem to mind providing a few extra details to liven up the recollection. That, I suppose, is the lasting appeal of nostalgia; the past isn't so intricately bound up with the details of reality; it's possible to look back and edit one's recollections, whereas the present has to be lived in the order and complexity with which it arrives. And at times anything seems better than now. Let's finish the chapter with another observation from Finley Peter Dunne:

The past always looks better than it was; it's only pleasant because it isn't here.

THE BRITISH CHARACTER.
A TENDENCY TO THINK THINGS NOT SO GOOD AS THEY USED
TO BE.

39

HEROISM

The Wreck.

The Lone Ranger and Tonto were riding through the prairie one day when they heard the sound of thundering hooves. It was the Cheyenne Indians, dressed in full warpaint and looking very mean. Our two heroes galloped on, but found their way ahead blocked by another huge band of Cheyenne. The Lone Ranger reined in his horse, Silver, turned to his trusty companion and said, 'Well, Tonto, looks as if we're going to have to shoot it out.'

Tonto looked at him. 'What do you mean — we — Paleface?'

'Sir, there's a Superhero outside.'
  'Who is it?'
  'The Invisible Man.'
  'Tell him I can't see him.'

A little boy is talking to his father. 'Daddy, what kind of a man does a soldier have to be, to be buried with full military honours?'
  'A dead one.'

An Irish infantry regiment was in the thick of battle during the First World War. 'Sir, sir,' a private shouted out to his Platoon Commander, 'we've run out of ammunition.'
  'We mustn't let the enemy know that,' says the officer. 'Whatever you do, keep firing.'

A big game hunter left his tent in the jungle one day without his gun and was confronted by an enormous lion preparing to spring. He froze and the animal leapt into the air, shot over his head and landed beyond him.

The hunter turned round to see the animal poised for another jump. Again it overshot the mark and landed beyond him. This continued for some time and eventually the hunter was able to crawl back into his tent.

When he emerged with his gun, he was amazed to see the lion on the other side of the clearing, practising little low jumps.

Did you hear about the Irish kamikaze pilot who was decorated after five hundred successful missions?

Come to that, did you hear about the Jewish kamikaze pilot who crashed his plane on top of his brother's scrap-yard?

We all need heroes. Whether you're a primitive tribesman hearing the annals of great warriors or a football supporter on the terraces, you want someone to look up to. And he can come from any walk of life. Thomas Carlyle:

The Hero can be Poet, Prophet, King, Priest or what you will, according to the kind of world he finds himself born into.

The important thing about a hero is that he's someone whose exploits we can admire and aspire to imitate, but never quite equal. As soon as we are as good as he is, that's the end. We have to go and look for another hero.

Some authorities believe that anyone is capable of heroism. For Matthew Arnold it was, like most things, a matter of will-power:

The will is free;
Strong is the soul, and wise, and beautiful;
The seeds of godlike power are in us still;
Gods are we, bards, saints, heroes, if we will.

Lord Chesterfield had a more pragmatic view of the subject:

I am convinced that a light supper, a good night's sleep, and a fine morning, have sometimes made a hero of the same man, who, by an indigestion, a restless night, and a raining morning would have proved a coward.

Ralph Waldo Emerson also favoured the demystification of heroism:

A hero is no braver than an ordinary man, but he is brave five minutes longer.

This cynical view of the claims of heroism is becoming increasingly prevalent, and there are many people who believe that heroes cannot exist in the modern world of computers and cornflakes. Part of the trouble in finding modern heroes is that war has been discredited as an honourable pastime and military glory was an important part of an old-fashioned hero's make-up. Two World Wars have tended to make people rather cynical.

Another basic drawback with heroism is that the traditional concept of the hero all too often involved dying an heroic death, which was, to say the least, inconvenient, and made it difficult for heroism to become a growth industry. And sometimes death could devalue the hero. Finley Peter Dunne:

> **No man is a hero to his undertaker.**

Oscar Wilde:

> **A thing is not necessarily true because a man dies for it.**

Havelock Ellis::

> **Heroes exterminate each other for the benefit of people who are not heroes.**

Possibly the most pointless (but heroic) way of dying is in a duel. Here's Mark Twain on the subject:

> **Much as the modern French duel is ridiculed by certain smart persons, it is in reality one of the most dangerous institutions of our day. Since it is nearly always fought in the open air, the contestants are nearly sure to catch cold.**

For a sample of the heroic death scene, let us turn to R. B. Sheridan's burlesque play, *The Critic*. Don Whiskerandos, the hero, is dying, watched by a Beefeater.

WHISKERANDOS: **And Whiskerandos quits this bustling scene**
For all eter- (*Dies*)
BEEFEATER: **Nity — he would have added, but stern death**
   Cut short his being, and the noun at once.

The dying bit, as a necessary qualification for heroic status, is still recognised in the twentieth century. Here's Will Rogers's view:

Being a hero is about the shortest-lived profession on earth.

But whereas, in classical times, death was welcomed if it brought glory, modern man is a little warier of what he lets himself in for. Here's an anonymous epigram:

> Soldiers who wish to be a hero
> Are practically zero,
> But those who wish to be civilians,
> Jesus, they run into millions.

So perhaps we need some guide-lines to help us recognise heroes in the modern age. Sheridan, again in *The Critic*, gave a useful tip for spotting the female variety:

> O Lord, sir, when a heroine goes mad, she always goes
> into white satin.

Charles Churchill, writing of an eighteenth-century actor, provided another useful clue:

> He's of stature somewhat low.
> Your hero always should be tall, you know.

While Dr Johnson also gave a hint for the recognition of heroic qualities:

> Claret is the liquor for boys; port for men; but he who
> aspires to be a hero must drink brandy.

One thing that every would-be hero must do to qualify is an heroic deed. But what would count as heroic nowadays? It was easy enough in the days of actual military engagements, fighting on against impossible odds. Everyone could recognise the heroism of that sort of thing. Here's a verse from *Chevy Chase*, a sixteenth-century poem by Richard Sheale:

> For Witterington needs must I wail,
> As one in doleful dumps;
> For when his legs were smitten off,
> He fought upon his stumps.

I suppose that must be a classic example of an heroic feat — or maybe just heroic feet. Here's more conspicuous gallantry, reported in the *Daily Mail:*

> Special praise to Petty Officer H. Robinson, gunnery
> instructor, who, when the guns jammed at one point,

took out his false teeth and threw them towards the Communists with an appropriate insult.

At the Battle of the River Plate, perhaps. Recently new forms of heroism have crept into military life. Here's a report from the *Evening News:*

To win a bet a soldier at Hadlow, Kent, fried a pair of clean woollen socks in a public house and ate them.

It's back to heroic feet again. But it doesn't bring us much nearer to defining a modern hero. Perhaps heroism is just imagination and retrospect and mankind isn't really suited to great deeds. Here's Dr Johnson's view:

It is thus that mutual cowardice keeps us in peace. Were one half of mankind brave and one half cowards, the brave would be always beating the cowards. Were all brave, they would lead a very uneasy life; all would be continually fighting; but being all cowards, we go on very well.

COURAGE.

Perhaps because so many of us are cowards, we have a diminishing effect on those who might have the seeds of heroism in them. Here's a thought on the subject from an anonymous American:

Hail the conquering hero comes,
Surrounded by a bunch of bums.

A problem with heroes — except for those considerate ones who achieve the final crown of an heroic death — is that they stay around for a long time. And no doubt write of their exploits. And certainly talk about them whenever they get the opportunity. In the words of Ralph Waldo Emerson:

Every hero becomes a bore at last.

Before he degenerates into boredom, there are advantages for the surviving hero. There's the adulation and respect of others, for a start. Here's a report from a wartime *Daily Telegraph:*

PATRIOTISM.

A popular padre in France is the Rev. H. Beauchamp, MC. He has a long record as a sportsman and he is also a fine ball-games player.

I hear that even now, at 62, he is proving that he is as good a rider across country as ever he was. Father Beauchamp's prowess and fine character have, I hear, so impressed the members of the officers' mess of a fighter squadron that they gave him their traditional accolade. This consisted of seizing him and holding him upside-down. Only those who meet with unqualified approval are subjected to this alarming honour.

Another supposed advantage of heroism is success with women. To the victor belong the spoils and, in Dryden's words:

None but the brave deserve the fair.

Unfortunately (or maybe fortunately for the less heroic amongst us) some women do not treat heroes with the respect that is their due. One such sad story is told in Thomas Hood's Pathetic Ballad, *Faithless Nellie Gray:*

Ben Battle was a soldier bold,
   And used to war's alarms;
But a cannon-ball took off his legs,
   So he laid down his arms.

Now as they bore him off the field,
   Said he, 'Let others shoot,
For here I leave my second leg,
   And the Forty-second Foot!'

The army surgeons made him limbs:
   Said he: 'They're only pegs;
But there's as wooden members quite
   As represent my legs!'

Now Ben he loved a pretty maid,
   Her name was Nèllie Gray:
So he went to pay her his devours
   When he'd devoured his pay!

But when he called on Nellie Gray,
    She made him quite a scoff;
And when she saw his wooden legs
    Began to take them off!

'O Nellie Gray! O Nellie Gray!
    Is this your love so warm?
The love that loves a scarlet coat
    Should be more uniform!'

She said, 'I loved a soldier once,
    For he was blythe and brave;
But I will never have a man
    With both legs in the grave!

'Before you had those timber toes,
    Your love I did allow,
But then, you know, you stand upon
    Another footing now!'

'Oh, false and fickle Nellie Gray;
    I know why you refuse:
Though I've no feet — some other man
    Is standing in my shoes!

I wish I ne'er had seen your face;
    But now, a long farewell!
For you will be my death, alas!
    You will not be my Nell!'

Now when he went from Nellie Gray,
    His heart so heavy got —
And life was such a burthen grown,
    It made him take a knot!

So round his melancholy neck,
    A rope he did entwine,
And, for his second time in life,
    Enlisted in the Line!

One end he tied around a beam,
    And then removed his pegs,
And as his legs were off — of course,
    He soon was off his legs!

49

And there he hung, till he was dead
    As any nail in town —
For though distress had cut him up,
    It could not cut him down!

A dozen men sat on his corpse,
    To find out why he died —
And they buried Ben in four cross-roads,
    With a *stake* in his inside!

And that really seems a fitting end to this chapter on heroism. I'm sure it still exists. I'm sure we're all capable of it. But perhaps we're all a bit like Tweedledum from *Alice Through the Looking Glass:*

I'm very brave generally... only today I happen to have a headache.

SUPERSTITION

THE DREAMER'S TRUE FRIEND.

CONTAINING NEARLY

1,000 DREAMS,

A medium at a seance gets a message for a widower who is sitting at the table. 'Arthur Barker, I believe this is your late wife knocking.'

'Ah,' says the man, 'she hasn't changed a bit.'

There was a man sitting in a railway compartment and he kept snapping his fingers. Snap, snap, snap, with monotonous regularity. It was getting on everyone's nerves and eventually the man opposite could not keep quiet any longer. 'Look, do you have to keep snapping your fingers?'

'Oh yes,' said the man, 'it keeps the tigers away.'

'But really,' blustered the irate commuter, 'there aren't any tigers in England.'

'See,' said the man, 'it works.'

'Oh-oh . . . I see the number thirteen. I hope you're not superstitious'

Two fortune tellers met on the sea-front. 'Ah,' said one, 'lovely weather, isn't it?'

'Yes,' said the other. 'Reminds me of the summer of 1997.'

A bus-conductress appeared in court charged with witchcraft. 'What happened exactly?' asked the judge.

'Well,' said the prosecuting council, 'when the bus arrived at the terminus, the accused shouted "All change" and the next thing she knew she had a bus full of frogs.'

A Victorian missionary in the wilds of Africa was determined to replace superstition with solid Victorian Christianity. So in the first tribe he came to he persuaded the entire adult population to go through proper Christian marriage ceremonies.

'There,' he said to the chief when the long task was over, 'don't you all feel better now you've been through the marriage service?'

'Oh yes,' replied the chief with a big grin. 'We've all got new wives.'

A woman went to a seance in hopes of getting in touch with her late husband who, during his life, had been a waiter in a big restaurant. The lights were dimmed, the medium went into a trance and the table began to make knocking sounds.

'Fred,' she said, 'Fred — is that you? Speak to me.'

'I can't,' said a ghostly voice. 'It's not my table.'

A nun was stopped at the Customs and the officer examined her luggage. 'And what's in this bottle, sister?' he asked.

'It's holy water,' she replied.

The Customs officer was suspicious, opened the bottle and sniffed it. 'That's not holy water,' he said. 'It's gin.'

'Lord be praised!' said the nun. 'A miracle!'

An old witch doctor's son went to England for a holiday and when he came back, his father asked him about English spells and superstitions. 'Oh,' said the boy, 'they have one marvellous ritual. It is called Cricket. A place of sacrifice is prepared with a roller and three ju-ju sticks are dug into the ground at either end. Then eleven men dressed in sacred white robes come out on to the sacred field. And then two more men, also in white, come out, bearing the mighty magic voodoo sticks. Then one of the priests takes a holy ball and throws it at the ju-ju sticks. And as soon as he starts doing that — the rains come pouring down!'

Superstition is a strange paradox. It's something that civilisations are always trying to grow out of, but it seems that as soon as they grow out of one set of superstitions, they replace them with a new lot. It's as if there's a constant desire for just so much irrational belief in our make-up, and some ideas will always get translated into folklore. In the words of T. H. Huxley:

> **It is the customary fate of new truths to begin as heresies and end as superstitions.**

Many superstitions remain unchanged for centuries. Indeed age is an essential part of superstition. Here's J. B. Morton's definition of the word:

> SUPERSTITION: **Noun accompanying the adjective medieval.**

There are plenty of people around today who pride themselves on their modern rational approach to life and yet will touch wood and think twice about walking under a ladder or leaving salt spilled on the table. The need for such observances is deep-rooted. There's a central weakness in us that requires such rituals. In the words of Edmund Burke:

> **Superstition is the religion of feeble minds.**

Its links with religion are close. Here's George Bernard Shaw on the subject:

> **No sooner had Jesus knocked over the dragon of superstition than Paul boldly set it on its legs again in the name of Jesus.**

However, few escape the attraction of superstition. Edmund Burke again:

> **In all superstition wise men follow fools.**

54

And you can't pretend the need for it isn't there. Francis Bacon:

There is a superstition in avoiding superstition.

It's amazing how much we consider the influence of luck in our lives. We spend a lot of time wishing each other luck, sending good luck cards and other charms. Here's a useful thing to send to a friend — depending of course on your choice of friends:

A piece of charmed coal — the burglar who carries this in his pocket will be strengthened against authority.

THE BRITISH CHARACTER.
PRONENESS TO SUPERSTITION.

Here's another useful tip from an old proverb:

> **He that would have good luck in horses must kiss the parson's wife.**

(I don't know who you have to kiss to have good luck with the parson's wife.)

Now let's have another superstition from Sir John Melton's *Astrologaster*, published in 1620:

> **If a man's nose bleeds one drop at the left nostril, it is a sign of good luck, and vice versa.**

(It doesn't say who it's good luck for. It sounds pretty bad luck for the man with the nose.)

The trouble is that the average person is not properly schooled in superstitions, so often does not actually know what is causing his good or bad fortune. A letter from the *Sunday Express:*

> **Are goldfish unlucky? A woman I met in a petshop told me that soon after she bought one her husband disappeared. Last week my son brought one home. Since then our cat, which we have had for several years, has vanished.**

Usually it's the other way round. You bring a cat home and the goldfish vanishes.

Many superstitions do have logical explanations. There is a theatrical one that it is unlucky to have live flowers on stage. Apart from the obvious economic and staffing problems of replacing them as they wilt, there is the danger that members of the cast might slip on fallen leaves. But it's harder to find sensible reasons why it's unlucky to quote from *Macbeth*, whistle in the dressing-room or write on a dressing-room mirror with make-up. And, in the more general area of superstitions there are many for which no explanation seems to make any sense. For example:

> **When you are buying onions, it is important to go to a shop with two doors. You must enter by one and go out of the other.**

As well as random beliefs, which defy systematic analysis, there are many complicated systems of superstition, by which omens can be read and fortunes predicted. There's reading of palms and cards and tea-leaves; there's phrenology and bibliomancy and hieromancy and

"Swearing on the horns at Highgate

9 Benjamin Stone

March 28ᵗʰ 1906

pyromancy and capnomancy and ornithomancy and pegomancy and aleuromancy and axinomancy and catoptromancy and more or less any other 'mancy' you care to invent. But probably the most popular form of divination, because of its regular appearance in the national press, is astrology.

It's difficult to know what to believe about the stars. I can see that there might be something in it when you have your own individual horoscope made up, but the sort of blanket coverage given in the newspapers does seem a bit dubious. I mean, if every single Taurean got news from abroad on the same day, how would the Post Office cope? And sometimes the advice given by Astrological Forecasters does seem excessively specific:

Those born about sunrise should wear wool next to their skin in winter and in summer. On the psychological front, they should avoid introspection like the plague.

57

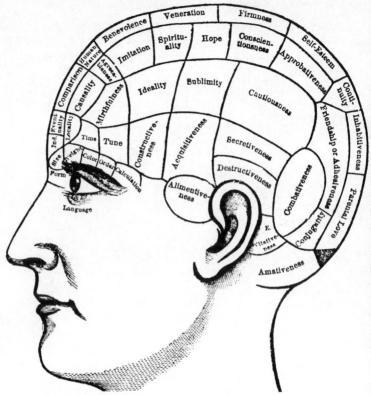

I suppose there are recognisable zodiacal types, but some of the generalisations about their characters do seem to be rather sweeping. An anonymous limerick:

> If Leo your own birthday marks,
> You will lust until forty, when starts
>   A new pleasure in stamps,
>   Boy Scouts and their camps,
> And fondling nude statues in parks.

And, while we're on astrological limericks, here's another from Tom St Brien:

> There once was a pretty Aquarian
> Got picked up by an octogenarian.
>   When he got her to bed,
>   'I'm a Leo,' he said,
> So she sent for the veterinarian.

Men have always been trying to foretell what's going to happen to them, and have yet to find a completely satisfactory method. And even if we did know the future, would it help? A poem by Sir John Suckling, entitled *Foreknowledge:*

> **If a man might know**
> **The ill he must undergo,**
> **And shun it so,**
> **Then it were good to know.**
>
> **But if he undergo it,**
> **Though he know it,**
> **What boots him know it?**
> **He must undergo it.**

The pointlessness of divination, by whatever method, is matched by its unreliability. Some enthusiasts set great store by the language of dreams, and whether they actually foreshadow events or not. There's a complex system of meanings in dreams and, if certain images appear in your dreams, certain results are supposed to ensue. Let's have a few examples of dream-objects and their meanings. Some have a kind of logic to them; others none at all:

> HEARSE — **You are about to have a very good time and a great deal of merry-making.**
> IDIOT — **You will be very successful in all your endeavours.**
> HEN — **You are about to have a very good time and a great deal of merry-making.**
> AXE — **A friend will help you out.**
> MURDER — **You will be very successful in all your endeavours.**
> BURIAL — **You will very shortly be married.**

There has long been suspicion of such methods of prediction. Here's the view of Thomas Nashe, writing in 1594:

> **Let but any man who is most conversant in the superstition of dreams reckon me one that hath happened just, and I'll set down a hundred out of histories that have perished to foolery. To come to late days. Louis XI dreamt that he swam in blood on the top**

of the Alps; which one Father Robert, a holy hermit of
his time, interpreted to be present death in his next wars
against Italy — though he lived and prospered in all his
enterprises a long while after.

Nashe didn't have much more respect for other forms of divination:

Just such-like imposture as is this art of exposition of
dreams are the arts of physiognomy and palmistry,
wherein who bearest most palm and praise is the
palpablest fool and crepundio. Lives there any such
slow, ice-brained, beef-witted gull, who by the rivelled
bark or outward rind of a tree will take upon him to
forespeak how long it shall stand, what mischances of
worms, caterpillars, boughs breaking, frost bitings,
cattle rubbing against it shall have? As absurd is it, by
the external branched seams or furrowed wrinkles in a
man's face or hand, in particular or general, to
conjecture and foredoom of his fate.
fate.

It's easy enough to scoff at stories of superstition set in the distant past or
in distant countries, because they have a tang of folksy unreality. But
superstitions are all around us and, as advances in the study of psychology
demonstrate the importance of will-power in the cure of illness, old
superstitious remedies don't seem much sillier than modern ones. If you
believe something works, then it probably does. Mind you, some
traditional remedies are a bit hard to swallow (and I mean that very
literally):

FOR THE CURE OF GALL-STONES — Boil sheep's dung with
new milk until it dissolves and drink the mixture.
FOR THE CURE OF THE AGUE -— Swallow a spider wrapped in
a raisin.
FOR THE CURE OF BEDWETTING — Children who cannot
retain their water should eat three roasted mice.

And then see how they run. Some people go for even less conventional
remedies. Here's a letter from *Picture Post:*

All who wish to be cured of carbuncle, gravel and
whatnot, and who desire luxurious bosoms, broccoli,
etc., should lie down on their faces from 7.18 to 7.33 p.m.

on June 23rd (the Feast of the Molars), reciting 'Arka, Arka, Tambouretta' while concentrating in thought on pottery and so on.

HEATHEN CEREMONIES ON THE RETURN OF THE PLEIADES.

A favourite form of superstition, apart from prediction and remedies, is trying to make contact with the dead. It's a very serious subject for those who believe in it, and has proved very useful to them. Here's a report from the *Brighton and Hove Gazette*:

During the last few years Miss Paxton has acted as a spiritual guide to a well-known MP. 'I go into a trance and compose his speeches for him,' she explained.

Quite a few MP's speeches sound as if they have been composed that way. But it's a dangerous business to meddle in, spiritualism. From the *Kensington Post:*

> **A woman who claims she is going to have a 'baby from Venus' has puzzled Mr George King, the leader of the Aetherius Society, which has its headquarters in the Fulham Road. 'I think she's been fiddling about with psychic matters,' says Mr King.**

And there can be more practical problems, as this *Sunday Express* report shows:

> **A Surrey man applying for new National Health spectacles said his old ones had been dematerialised at a spiritualist seance.**

Seances do produce results for those who believe in them, but the dead seem most commonly to manifest themselves by tapping tables or moving glasses. Physical materialisation is much rarer, though the world is full of stories of ghosts walking. Mind you, it must be a bit of a shock when it happens. Here's a poem by Thomas Hood:

SALLY SIMPKIN'S LAMENT; or JOHN JONES'S KIT-KAT-ASTROPHE

'Oh! what is that comes gliding in,
  And quite in middling haste?
It is the picture of my Jones,
  And painted to the waist.

'It is not painted to the life,
  For where's the trowsers blue?
Oh Jones, my dear! — Oh dear! my Jones,
  What is become of you?'

'Oh! Sally dear, it is too true, —
  The half that you remark
Is come to say my other half
  Is bit off by a shark!

'Oh! Sally, sharks do things by halves,
  Yet most completely do!
A bite in one place seems enough,
  But I've been bit in two.

'You know I once was all your own,
  But now a shark must share!
But let that pass — for now, to you
  I'm neither here nor there.

'Alas! death has a strange divorce
  Effected in the sea,
It has divided me from you,
  And even me from me!

'Don't fear my ghost will walk o'nights
  To haunt, as people say;
My ghost *can't* walk, for, oh! my legs
  Are many leagues away!

'Lord! think when I am swimming round,
  And looking where the boat is,
A shark just snaps away a *half*,
  Without "a *quarter's* notice".

        .

'One half is here, the other half
   Is near Columbia placed;
Oh! Sally, I have got the whole
   Atlantic for my waist.

'But now, adieu — a long adieu!
   I've solved death's awful riddle,
And would say more, but I am doomed
   To break off in the middle!'

The modern superstition is that we're free of superstition, but it doesn't fit the facts. There seem to be as many strange beliefs around as ever before, at least if the papers are anything to go by. This is from the *Sunday Express:*

In Lancashire it is still believed by many women that if they want to have a male child their husbands must wear boots at the time of conception.

A letter to a woman's magazine:

I am expecting my first baby in two months from now. We have a little kitten which I am always playing with, but friends tell me I should not, or my baby will be hairy. Is this true?

And here's one from a letter in the *Daily Mail:*

All my life I have suffered from very hairy ears. Two years ago a friend told me that this was because I was a Liberal... This so impressed me that I joined the Socialist Party, and now I have very hairy backs to my hands too.

So long as people can believe in things like that, who dares say that superstition is dead?

BRÉTON WOMEN STREWING THE SEA WITH FLOWERS.

BOREDOM

A bloke I know has a very low threshold of boredom, but at last he got a job that really suited him — testing mattresses in a bed factory. He didn't stay, mind. Couldn't stand the way they kept waking him up for tea-breaks.

Then the same bloke got another job — working on a building site. After a couple of days he and his mate went to the foreman to ask for more shovels. 'You've got plenty,' said the foreman. 'If you're short, you can lean against each other.'

'Would you say the vicar's sermon this morning was inspiring?'
  'Oh yes — as soon as he'd finished preaching, a great awakening came over the congregation.'

A psychiatrist looked with despair at his patient, a young girl, who was sitting apathetically in the chair in his consulting-room. 'Look, this can't go on,' he said. 'It's six months now that you've been coming to see me. I keep on trying to console you, to reassure you, to get you to take a different view of life. But you just sit there sighing and hardly say a word. Why?'
  'Well, doctor,' she replied, 'You're so boring, aren't you?'

A lecturer cornered one of his students in the corridor. 'Well, and how did you enjoy my lecture?'
  'I thought it was very interesting,' replied the student politely.
  'Any criticisms at all?'
  'Well...' the student pondered. 'Perhaps it was a bit long.'
  'Long?'
  Desperately the student tried to extricate himself. 'No, no, I didn't mean it *was* long. I just meant it *seemed* long.'

A golf bore made his girlfriend caddy for him for a complete round. Then he took her back to the clubhouse and, over a drink, went through his round hole by hole, analysing every shot. Finally he could see that she was getting rather bored and decided magnanimously that it was her turn to talk. 'Tell me, darling,' he said, 'what did *you* think of my drive at the eleventh?'

A farmer made his annual trip to a boring little market town and sold his entire year's produce. His pockets bulging with money, he wandered round the town looking for somewhere to celebrate. But it was after eight o'clock in the evening, everything seemed to be locked up and everyone in bed. At last he met a woman walking along the deserted street. 'Excuse me,' he said, 'where's the night-life in this town?'

'I am,' she replied.

The resort we went to on holiday last year was so boring. Nothing happened. Even the tide didn't go out after six. The only late-night entertainment was watching the traffiic-lights change. And the people were so quiet too. A bloke sat in the hotel lounge for three weeks before anyone realised he was dead.

A young wife was asked by her friend what she thought of married life. 'Oh, it doesn't make a lot of difference,' she replied. 'Still pretty boring. I used to wait up half the night for George to go home, and now I wait up half the night for him to come home.'

'Put me down as apathetic if you like—
it makes no difference to me'

70

Everyone at some stage in life has been utterly, impossibly, excruciatingly bored. Sometimes the state is imposed by external circumstances, like work, or being laid up in bed, or missing a train. More often it is inflicted by other people.

Everyone knows a lot of bores. It's one of those strange qualities, though, that doesn't work in the first person. If you decline the verb 'to be a bore', it goes : 'you are a bore' — 'he is a bore' — 'they are bores'. You very rarely hear 'I am a bore'. It's a terrible thought actually — even the most crushing bore in the world thinks he's being interesting. It's a blinkered view, but one from which we all suffer at times. Here's a definition by Ambrose Bierce:

BORE, n. A person who talks when you wish him to listen.

La Rochefoucauld:

We often forgive those who bore us, but we cannot forgive those whom we bore.

Oliver Wendell Holmes:

All men are bores, except when we want them.

H. L. Mencken:

The capacity of human beings to bore one another seems to be vastly greater than that of any other animal. Some of their most esteemed inventions have no other apparent purpose; for example, the dinner party of more than two, and the science of metaphysics.

71

But bores are undaunted by such thoughts. Most continue secure in the unfounded assumption that whatever they talk about is of enormous interest to their listeners. Though in some cases, their efforts take on the stature of an art. Sir Walter Scott, who was no mean bore himself, wrote:

It requires no small talents to be a decided bore.

But, of course, the decided bore must be oblivious to his own tedium. Robert Lynd:

Many bores are so obviously happy that it is a pleasure to watch them.

Mind you, there are tricks for being really successfully boring. Voltaire revealed the most important one:

The secret of being a bore is to tell everything.

That is it — the one great quality all bores have in common — a grasp of detail. They don't let you escape a single fact. In fact, amongst bores, there is a complete language of amplification. Whereas most people just supply basic information in reply to questions bores give so much more. Let's examine some examples of Borese:

QUESTION	ANSWER IN ENGLISH	ANSWER IN BORESE
Who's your friend?	Someone from work	**Well, he's a fellow who's in the same line of country as me and lives in the same neck of the woods actually, and the interesting thing about him is that his wife's cousin once met my wife's aunt in Malta.**
How did you get here?	Along the bypass	**Ah, well, we took the A20 out of town, then went down the A224, joined the A2, turned off down the B2042 and — Bob's your uncle — there we were on the B269.**
How are you?	OK	**Well, I had a touch of 'flu last week — still feeling a bit under the weather — you know, the glands — and the tummy hasn't quite settled down — my leg's playing up a bit too and...**

And so on and so on and so on...

It's not just people who are potentially boring. Sometimes a situation can be. Traditionally, the country is supposed to be less stimulating than the town. The Reverend Sydney Smith:

I have no relish for the country; it is a kind of healthy grave.

Another thought on the same subject from the same source:

It is a place with only one post a day... In the country I always fear that creation will expire before tea-time.

Something that's a source of boredom to all of us is officialdom and petty regulation. It's easy to imagine offices full of little men spinning red tape and producing nonsense with authority. Let's look at some examples of regulations at work from the late 'forties. First, from the *News Chronicle:*

Acrobats have been classified as sedentary workers, and are not entitled to extra bread coupons.

From the National Insurance Act:

For the purpose of the Part of this Schedule a person over pensionable age, not being an insured person, shall be treated as an employed person if he would be an insured person were he under pensionable age and would be an employed person were he an insured person.

Finally, a letter from the *Daily Telegraph:*

Having had a leg amputated during the war I am, as a cripple, allowed an extra ration of soap. On producing a doctor's certificate to the effect that I only had one leg I was supplied with the extra coupons. These coupons becoming exhausted, I applied for a further supply, only to be told that I must produce a further certificate to the effect that my leg is still off.

THERE was a young Lady of Bude
Who was horribly bored by a dude,
    Till she gave him a hint
    That was plainer than print—
And a desperate silence ensued.

All those regulations are the proud products of boring little men in offices. A lot of them are probably commuters, driven mad by the tedium of their daily journey. Here's a poetic definition by E. B. White:

> **Commuter — one who spends his life**
> **In riding to and from his wife;**
> **A man who shaves and takes a train**
> **And then rides back to shave again.**

'I'm sick to death of being a bureaucrat. I'd resign tomorrow if I only knew the correct procedure.'

Marriage is an estate that is often abused as being boring and that's a criticism that's been around as long as the institution has existed. Here's an anonymous eighteenth-century verse:

'My dear, what makes you always yawn?'
The wife exclaimed, her temper gone;
'Is home so dull and dreary?'
'Not so, my love,' he said, 'not so;
But man and wife are one, you know,
And when alone I'm weary.'

It's possible to break the monotony of home life by going out for the evening, but that doesn't always work. Entertainment is not always as entertaining as it should be. A report from a wartime *Daily Telegraph:*

ENSA describes as without foundation an allegation by an actor at a British Equity meeting that members of the Forces have had to be locked in at its performances.

One often gets the feeling, reading between the lines of newspapers' Entertainment pages, that entertainment may be a misnomer. From the *Star:*

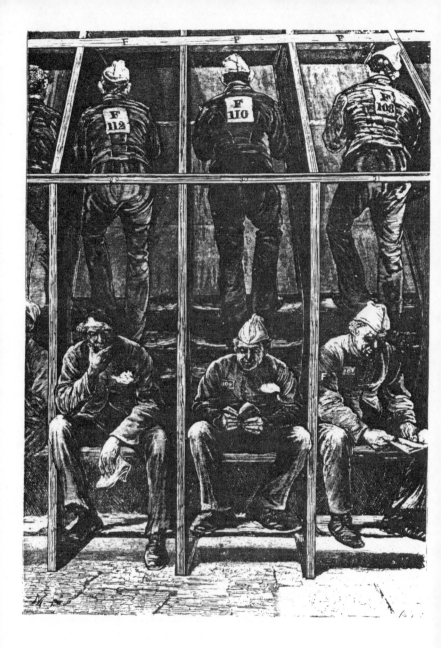

I admired the skill with which she sang. 'I Can't Give You Anything But Love, Baby' in French and made it sound like another number altogether.

From a Surrey paper:

> Miss Jennings has been specially engaged for the Festival and cannot be in London again before June 9th — all of which is highly satisfactory.

And a note from a Choir Festival programme:

> To relieve the monotony of sitting, the audience are asked to rise during the rendering of the Chorus, 'Fix'd in His everlasting seat'.

There are some jobs which always sound boring and among them is weather forecasting. I'm sure it's a fascinating business if you're in it, but, to the outsider, weathermen always sound rather bored. Perhaps it's just the voice that goes with the job, touched with a note of resignation to the fact that half the audience don't believe you and are longing to see you proved wrong. Some weather reports are pretty unbelievable anyway. From an Irish paper:

> Forecast for today: Winds freshening, fair at first, apart from fog, becoming cloudy or dull, and milk with local rain or drizzle later.

And from the *Monmouth (Illinois) Review Atlas*:

> Blizzard-like weather moved in from the southwest along about midnight last night, and those who sleep light said there were high guests starting about midnight and reaching a peak around two in the morning.

Yes, we've all heard them. Slamming their car doors, revving their engines, and always coming from the party you weren't invited to. Guests can of course be boring as well as noisy. A thought from William Dean Howells:

> Some people can stay longer in an hour than others can in a week.

It usually depends on how much they talk. And what they talk about. Idealists can be particularly wearing with their everlasting earnestness. A verse from G. K. Chesterton's *Ballad of an Anti-Puritan:*

> They spoke of progress spiring round,
>   Of Light and Mrs Humphrey Ward —
> It is not true to say I frowned,
>   Or ran about the room and roared;
> I might have simply sat and snored —
>   I rose politely in the club
> And said, 'I feel a little bored;
>   Will someone take me to a pub?'

One can also get extremely bored listening to lectures. They can go on a bit. A report from the *Bangor (Maine) Daily News:*

> **William P. MacKaye gave an illustrated lecture on 'The Romance of Coffee'. Tea was served by the hostesses.**

Another one from a Nebraska newspaper:

> **Dean S. P. Swenson came through sensationally in his high school talk, packing as smartly-contrived a 10-minute speech into 20 minutes as this town has recently heard.**

I think we have all heard speeches of that sort. The ones to be wary of are those that begin, 'Ladies and gentlemen, I'm not going to speak for long...' Having raised your hopes in this way, they are usually interminable. It's the same in popular music when a singer says, 'One more time'. It always means at least three more times, and often more.

'There he goes again with his mad craving for excitement'

Public speaking can be a form of torture for the audience. Sydney Smith certainly thought so when he wrote of someone:

[He] deserves to be preached to death by wild curates.

Anything that goes on too long becomes boring in time, so I think I will avoid the danger and end my chapter here. With just one closing thought — from a Calcutta newspaper:

A very fitting end to a very wet afternoooon came when Mrs K——— gave away the prizes.

'There must be something out there you haven't vandalised.'

PRIDE

WHO'LL FIGHT FOR THE QUEEN?

WRITTEN AND COMPOSED BY

GEORGE LINLEY.

LONDON.

A Texan was boasting to an Englishman about his vast estate back home. 'Do you know, it takes me a whole day to drive round it.'

'Oh yes,' said the Englishman. 'I had a car like that once.'

There were two businessmen who were great rivals and kept vying with each other by buying more and more status symbols. One bought a swimming pool; the other bought a larger swimming pool. One bought a Bentley; the other bought a Rolls-Royce. The first man was determined to go one better, so he had a telephone installed in his Bentley and, all set to show off, rang up his rival. There was no reply at the man's home and the call was transferred to the Rolls-Royce. Then he heard his rival's voice saying, 'Hello. Can you hang on a minute? I'm on the other line.'

A golfer and his caddie were tramping through the woods looking for a ball. Eventually the caddie stopped. 'I'm sorry, sir. I'm lost.'

'Lost! What do you mean?' shouted the golfer. 'I thought you were supposed to be the best caddie in the club.'

'I am,' said the caddie, 'and proud of it. But we left the club ten minutes ago.'

A lecturer in the Highlands of Scotland was boasting of his ancestry. 'I was born an Englishman, I live as an Englishman and I hope to die as an Englishman.'

'Ach,' said a voice from the back of the hall. 'Have ye nae ambition at all?'

A man goes to the psychiatrist and says, 'I suppose I am remarkable in that I always get my own way. I'm enormously ambitious and totally selfish. Whatever I want—women, possessions, power, money — I just go out and get it. I won't take no for an answer. I just go out and get it, regardless of others.'

'Hmm,' said the psychiatrist. 'And how long have you had this complaint?'

'Who's complaining?'

At a football match a very conceited centre-forward missed an open goal. 'Oh dear,' he said, 'I'm not playing my usual game.'

'Oh,' said the opposing full-back, 'what game's that?'

THE BRITISH CHARACTER.
REFUSAL TO ADMIT DEFEAT.

An Englishman and a Scotsman were arguing about the respective merits of their two countries. 'Oh, come on,' said the Englishman, 'look at Scotland. Take away the mountains and the lochs and all that scenery and what have you got left?'

'England,' said the Scot.

A Methodist minister, a Catholic priest and a rabbi were talking. 'One of my ancestors wrote two hundred hymns,' boasted the Methodist.

'One of my ancestors wrote a revised version of the Bible,' countered the Catholic.

The rabbi said, 'Just cool it, you two. Who do you think wrote the Ten Commandments?'

An American was boasting to an Irish labourer about the height of sky-scrapers in his country and said that some of them were so high you could never see the top for cloud.

'That's nothing,' said the Irishman. 'I was once working on a building in Dublin that was so high, when I dropped me hammer on the Friday, I didn't realise it till it fell on me head on me way into work on the Monday.'

We all puff up with a bit of pride sometimes. However much modesty forbids us to assert it, there is a little bit of us for which we have a sneaking affection, a bit that we really think is rather better than anything other people can offer. But it doesn't do to admit it. Mark Twain:

Good breeding consists in concealing how much we think of ourselves and how little we think of the other person.

It's silly, really, this convention of modesty, but it's very much part of the English character. We are by nature self-effacing and only hint at our real brilliance. But pride does insulate us, keep us distinct from the mediocrity of the rest of the world. A definition from Ambrose Bierce's *Devil's Dictionary:*

EGOTIST, n. A person of low taste, more interested in himself than in me.

We all deserve better treatment. William Shakespeare:

Vanity keeps persons in favour with themselves who are out of favour with all others.

Robert Louis Stevenson:

Vanity dies hard; in some obstinate cases it outlives the man.

Arnold Bennett:

It is a profound truth that women as a sex are vain; it is also a profound truth that men as a sex are vain.

There are plenty of people around who are just cocky, but to attain true style one needs more than cockiness; sheer, blind arrogance is what's needed. Let's have a few sublimely arrogant remarks. Oscar Wilde at the New York Custom House:

I have nothing to declare except my genius.

The statesman Metternich:

I cannot help saying to myself twenty times a day, 'My God, how right I am.'

'This could have been written for me'

Benjamin Disraeli:

When I want to read a book, I write one.

Such remarks have to be delivered with enormous panache and confidence. Some writers are very good at them. Here's another which Oscar Wilde put into the mouth of one of his characters in *An Ideal Husband* (though I bet he said it himself first):

> **'Other people are quite dreadful. The only possible society is oneself.'**

George Bernard Shaw was no slouch at this sort of remark:

> **My speciality is being right when other people are wrong.**

Or again:

> **I often quote myself; it adds spice to my conversation.**

People who lack the wit and confidence for that sort of arrogant phrase-making have other sources of pride. Titles, for example. Another definition from Abrose Bierce:

> **PRIDE, n. Refusing to pay your tailor's bill, because he addressed you as 'Mr' instead of 'Esq'.**

Here's a report from the *Evening Standard*:

> **Westminster City Council's rat-catcher, Mr Hopper, is in future to be called Rodent Officer.**

Very proper. Another from the *Edinburgh Evening Dispatch*:

> **In her dread of the 'public scandal' that would be produced by the birth of a baby within four months of her son's marriage, it must be confessed that the pursuer's mother had the support of her husband, who betrayed in the witness box a somewhat ludicrous sense of his own importance in the public life of Edinburgh as the layer of main gas pipes.**

As you reach a certain status in life, it is important to surround yourself with objects fitting to your dignity. An advertisement from *The Pioneer*:

> **FOR SALE — Cottage piano made in Berlin, owner getting grand.**

90

People have been 'getting grand' for as long as there have been people about. Alexander Pope called pride 'the never-failing vice of fools' and it has, from classical times on, provided good material for epigrams. Here's Thomas Heywood, writing in the sixteenth century about a proud man:

> He standeth well in his own conceit each man tells;
> So had he need, for he standeth in no man's else.

Here's a seventeenth-century one by Barten Holyday:

> Pride cannot see itself by mid-day light:
> The peacock's tail is furthest from his sight!

And another from Thomas Moore in the nineteenth century, about one Marcus:

> Of all speculations the market holds forth,
>   The best that I know for a lover of pelf
> Is to buy Marcus up, at the price he is worth,
>   And then sell him at that which he sets on himself.

El David Dess Paris

Imp Lemercier &Cⁱᵉr de Seine 57 Paris

"Dᵣ Livingstone I presume ! „

PORTRAIT GALLERY OF BRITISH COSTUME

October 1872

Published with the TAILOR AND CUTTER by JOHN WILLIAMSON 93, Drury Lane London W.C.

No amount of argument can persuade that sort of person that he isn't God's gift to everything. It must be rather pleasant to have that sort of conceit. Like this character, described by Arnold Bennett:

His opinion of himself, having once risen, remained at 'set fair'.

Women are traditionally accused of vanity, especially in matters of appearance. Women's Lib may have produced a more natural and less made-up woman, but the majority are still very concerned about looking their best. And attaining that state may involve enlisting a little artificial aid. An anonymous eighteenth-century epigram — *On a Lady Who Was Painted*:

It sounds a paradox — and yet 'tis true,
You're like your picture, though 'tis not like you.

Salvador Dali came up with a similar thought, but a totally different meaning:

> I do not paint a portrait to look like a subject, rather does the person grow to look like his portrait.

(Considering Dali's type of painting, there must be some pretty odd-looking people walking about.) More on the subject of women's make-up from Percy Bysshe Shelley:

> To youths, who hurry thus away,
> How silly your desire is —
> At such an early hour to pay
> Your compliments to Iris.
>
> Stop, prithee, stop, ye hasty beaux,
> No longer urge this race on;
> Though Iris has put on her clothes,
> She has not put her face on.

Snobbery is a form of pride and the respect for ancestry is no less now than it has ever been. The farther back your family goes, the better. From Gilbert and Sullivan's *The Mikado*:

> I can trace my ancestry back to a protoplasmal primordial atomic globule. Consequently, my family pride is something inconceivable. I can't help it. I was born sneering.

And people of the right background keep on sneering, however their circumstances change. A letter from the old *Sunday Dispatch*:

> I am of royal blood, being a direct descendant of the kings of Munster. Unfortunately I married below my station — my husband has an iron-mongery business and we live in Wimbledon. Most of our neighbours are vulgar people, and I long for more fastidious friends and surroundings. I have a natural sense of dignity. How can I get back where I belong?

If you can't actually trace your own ancestry back, you can still keep your pride nourished by contact with those who can. And that's true whoever you are. From a wartime edition of the *Bournemouth Times*:

> Fishing in a local stream the day before the visit of the
> King and Queen to Canford School, the headmaster
> caught a three-pound brown trout. He offered it to the
> Queen, who was very pleased to accept it, and carried it
> back to London with her. It was put in her car and
> wrapped up in the *Bournemouth Times*. She probably
> had it for her dinner that night. A cat may look at a king,
> but it's a lucky brown trout that gets eaten by a Queen.

And I hope the trout was properly aware of the honour.

Another source of pride is knowledge and education. Though it is wise to temper such thoughts with a little humility. Here's a sixteenth-century epigram by John Heath:

> All things you know; what all? If it be so,
> Then you know this too, that you nothing know.

I think it could be time for a cautionary tale on the evils of pride, from the works of Hilaire Belloc:

> GODOLPHIN HORNE,
> *Who was cursed with the Sin of Pride, and Became a
> Boot-Black.*
>
> Godolphin Horne was Nobly Born;
> He held the Human Race in scorn,
> And lived with all his Sisters where
> His father lived, in Berkeley Square.
> And oh! the Lad was Deathly Proud!
> He never shook your Hand or Bowed,
> How perfectly ridiculous!
> Alas! That such Affected Tricks
> Should flourish in a Child of Six!
> (For such was Young Godolphin's age).
> Just then, the Court required a Page,
> Whereat the Lord High Chamberlain
> (The Kindest and the Best of Men),
> He went good-naturedly and took
> A Perfectly Enormous Book
> Called *People Qualified to Be
> Attendant on His Majesty*,
> And murmured, as he scanned the list
> (To see that no one should be missed),

TO THE GLORIOUS
MEMORY OF
GENERAL
SIR HILARY
MARTINET-FUDDY
G.C.B.

ERECTED THROUGH THE
VOLUNTARY CONTRIBUTIONS
OF
PRIVATE SOLDIERS

THE PRIVATE MAUSOLEUM
OF
THE
THREEP-POTTLE FAMILY

NO CONNECTION
WITH ANY OTHER
GRAVE IN THIS
CEMETERY

AMY
POTTLE
1888-1956

R.I.P

'There's William Coutts has got the 'Flu,
And Billy Higgs would never do,
And Guy de Vere is far too young,
And... wasn't D'Alton's Father hung?
And as for Alexander Byng! — ...
I think I know the kind of thing,
A Churchman, cleanly, nobly born,
Come let us say Godolphin Horne?'
But hardly had he said the word
When Murmurs of Dissent were heard.
The King of Iceland's Eldest Son
Said, 'Thank you! I am taking none!'
The Aged Duchess of Athlone
Remarked, in her sub-acid tone,
'I doubt if He is what we need!'
With which the Bishops all agreed;
And even Lady Mary Flood
(*So* kind, and oh! so *really* good)
Said, 'No! He wouldn't do at all,
He'd make us feel a lot too small.'
The Chamberlain said, '... Well, well, well!
No doubt you're right... One cannot tell!'
He took his Gold and Diamond Pen
And scratched Godolphin out again.
So now Godolphin is the Boy
Who blacks the Boots at the Savoy.

National pride is not as strong as it might be in these degenerate days, but there was a time when people knew what it meant to be British. A. M. Lowe from a wartime *Daily Sketch:*

Great Britain has been responsible for nearly every major invention which has proved of benefit to the world.

I like the touch of modesty in the word 'nearly'. Another burst of patriotism from a letter to the *Manchester Evening News:*

> When one reads sports news these days one invariably comes across the parrot phrase 'tough as teak', especially in boxing. Cannot our writers occasionally remind us that there are woods of our own country which are tougher than the coconut brown? I suggest they refer to such timbers as ash, oak, beech, birch, when they want to emphasise the toughness of some of our British manhood.

An important part of the whole mechanism of pride is the possession of status-symbols. It is really thought to matter the sort of house you live in and the sort of car you own. Cars are particularly important. A report from the *Daily Mail*:

> **A fish-fryer who wanted a Rolls-Royce to carry guests at his daughter's wedding at fashionable St Ann's church was today awarded five guineas damages as compensation when 'inferior' cars were supplied.**

And a rather sad little advertisement from *The Times*:

> **Sports car, preferably foreign, wanted week-end 22nd June by respectable middle-aged civil servant to raise son's status at preparatory school where most fathers have Jaguars.**

And that pretty well winds up my look into the subject of pride. I'll close with a couple of quick thoughts. First, from George Ade:

> **A man never feels more important than when he receives a telegram containing more than ten words.**

And from Wyndham Lewis:

> **It is the proud perpetual boast of the Englishman that he never brags.**

JEALOUSY

I wouldn't say my wife's jealous, but she's the only woman I know!

A man went to the casualty department of a hospital with a bloodstained handkerchief round his finger. A pretty nurse went across to him and unwrapped the finger to reveal a very deep cut. Immediately she burst into tears and, holding the hand to her face, wept piteously over it for several minutes.

When she had stopped and the man had gone to get the wound stitched up, another nurse asked, 'Why did you cry? He wasn't very badly hurt.'

'He jilted me last year for another woman,' replied the girl. 'I was crying to get salt in the cut.'

'You said your wife was angry when she found a letter in your pocket. Was it one you'd forgotten to post?'

'No, it was one I'd forgotten to burn.'

A newly-married couple were sitting in the pub when a gorgeous blonde slunk past. 'Hello, Nigel darling,' she purred as she went by.

'Who was that?' asked the wife immediately.

'I wish you'd stop asking awkward questions,' her husband replied. 'I'm going to have enough trouble explaining who you are.'

'Oh,' said one little boy to another, 'I wish I was rich. I'd give a thousand pounds to be one of them millionaires.'

There's a lot of jealousy between the different branches of the Armed Forces. When the RAF developed planes that could go faster than sound, the Army started working on a sound that could go faster than planes.

A young bride on her honeymoon said to her husband, 'Now I want you to sack your secretary.'

'But why?' the husband remonstrated. 'After all, you used to be my secretary yourself.'

'That's why.'

'Darling,' said the young man to his girlfriend, 'you're a girl in a thousand.'

She burst into tears. 'Have there been that many before?'

A Scot and a Jew went into business together and bought a second-hand bus. They agreed that the Scot should drive and the Jew should collect the fares. The Jew was very happy with the arrangement and immediately insured the Scot for £5,000. A week later the Scot was dead of a twisted neck.

The Jew collected the insurance, bought two more buses, got his two brothers into the business, and advertised for three Scotsmen able to drive.

Two young wives are talking. One says to the other, 'Does your husband talk in his sleep?'

'No. He just grins. It's exasperating.'

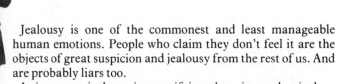

Jealousy is one of the commonest and least manageable human emotions. People who claim they don't feel it are the objects of great suspicion and jealousy from the rest of us. And are probably liars too.

At its worst, jealousy is a terrifying obsession and at its best it's still pretty unattractive. A few thoughts on the subject. First, from John Churton Collins:

> **Envy and fear are the only passions to which no pleasure is attached.**

La Rochefoucauld:

> **Envy is more irreconcilable than hatred.**

A verse from Ecclesiasticus in the *Apocrypha:*

> **Envy and wrath shorten the life.**

Most human evils will yield to the power of reason, but jealousy is very resistant to it. Some lines from *Othello*, the great tragedy of jealousy:

> **But jealous souls will not be answered so;**
> **They are not ever jealous for the cause,**
> **But jealous for they are jealous.**

And they are jealous of absolutely anything. A character described by Wodroephe, writing in 1623:

> **He would have flayed a louse for her skin, he was so covetous.**

Here's a personification of Envy taken from *Pierce Penniless, his Supplication to the Devil*, published by Thomas Nashe in 1592:

Envy is a crocodile that weeps when he kills, and fights with none but he feeds on. This is the nature of this quick-sighted monster: he will endure any pains to endamage another, waste his body with undertaking exploits that would require ten men's strengths, rather than any should get a penny but himself, blear his eyes to stand in his neighbours light, and, to conclude, like Atlas underprop heaven alone, rather than any should be in heaven that he liked not of, or come unto heaven by any other means but by him.

The Duke of Gloucester goes into mourning for his little Nephews.

A jealous person is suspicious of everyone. He doesn't like the idea of anyone having something that he hasn't got. Oscar Wilde:

> **Anyone can sympathise with the sufferings of a friend, but it requires a very fine nature to sympathise with a friend's success.**

Some people find it quite intolerable to see another getting better treatment than they are, whatever the circumstances. An epigram from the Latin of Gaius Lucilius:

> **Diophon was being crucified,**
> **But when he saw another near him on a higher cross**
> **He died of envy.**

And a comment from Robert Burton:

> **Like Aesop's fox, when he had lost his tail, would have all his fellow foxes cut off theirs.**

Yes, a jealous character likes to see everyone suffering under equal disadvantages, or preferably slightly greater disadvantages than his own. He is a killjoy and expresses his jealousy in disapproval. A report from the *Daily Sketch*:

> **The Councillor told Windsor Council's general purposes committee meeting: 'I was shocked at the lack of morals. There were young girls having their navels and breasts painted with flowers in broad daylight. At night couples were carrying on acts of immorality. I was in the Guards and I know what they were up to.'**

Jealousy is by definition an ungenerous emotion and one that aims at exclusive ownership. Here's an example of it at work from the *Hampstead and Highgate Express*:

> **The Inspector presiding at the enquiry, Mr V. D. Joll, asked: 'Will there be any free water closets?'**
> **Mr Hudson: 'Sir, all water closets in Hampstead are free.'**
> **A member of the public: 'So we ratepayers are paying for the convenience of people who may come from other boroughs?'**

Though jealousy in matters of material possessions is strong, it is far stronger in affairs of love. Indeed, Ambrose Bierce provides this definition:

JEALOUSY, n. **The seamy side of love.**

It has long been accepted as an essential part of the make-up of the young lover, and leads to many tears and arguments. Young people are particularly susceptible when they start to go out to parties and meet members of the opposite sex. A sad story related in a letter to *Woman's Mirror:*

> **I went to a dance which was started off with the guests being given a label bearing the name of half a well-known dish. You had to find the person with the other half. For instance, fish went with chips, roast beef with Yorkshire pudding, and so on. My label was egg, and I found a boy labelled bacon, but when I spoke to him he said, 'Let's have a look round first.' Then he went off with a girl labelled liver and I was left with nobody except a boy labelled onions, which certainly didn't go with egg.**

Unfortunately, maturity doesn't bring an end to jealousy in affairs of the heart. In fact, it gets worse. In the words of Horner, the hero of Wycherley's *The Country Wife:*

> **As gout in age from pox in youth proceeds,**
> **So, wenching past, then jealousy succeeds;**
> **The worst disease that love and wenching breeds.**

Women's jealousy is proverbial for its strength. In the oft-misquoted words of William Congreve:

> **Heav'n has no rage, like love to hatred turn'd,**
> **Nor Hell a fury, like a woman scorn'd.**

The point is again made by Arthur Wing Pinero:

> **All jealous women are mad.**

And Matthew Prior:

For story and experience tell us
That man grows old and woman jealous.

Some women are so jealous that they can't bear the thought of their men bringing home any influences from the world outside. Here's a description of one such by Caecilius:

She'd have you spew up what you'd drunk abroad.

Male and female jealousy have their most violent clashes in the setting of marriage. Many violent marital rows are caused by the unfaithfulness or, just as often, the supposed unfaithfulness of one partner or the other. The danger of a man choosing too beautiful a wife is one of the most popular themes of early literature. Here's John Florio on the subject:

> He that a white horse and a fair wife keepeth,
> For fear, for care, for jealousy scarce sleepeth.

The cuckold is a traditional figure of fun — the unsuspecting husband with the unfaithful wife. A little verse now by Matthew Prior:

> When Pontius wished an edict might be passed
> That cuckolds should into the sea be cast,
> His wife, assenting, thus replied to him:
> 'But first, my dear, I'd have you learn to swim.'

And another equally cynical one, by an anonymous poet:

> Tom found a trinket in his bed,
> Which he'd to Stephen's mistress given;
> 'What's this, dear wife?' 'Only' (she said)
> 'Your gift to Ann — returned by Stephen.'

'Frankly, I don't know how much longer I can stand the certainty of being the Only Woman.'

Wife-swapping has been around for a long time. It's a practice that leads to many marital problems — not to mention simple practical complications. A report from — where else? — *The People:*

> **The husband added that their wife-swapping activities were restricted in the summer because he played cricket at weekends.**

Promiscuity almost always leads to jealousy on someone's part, and sexual jealousy can be an appallingly strong emotion. It leads to scenes of frightening violence. A paragraph from the *Edinburgh Evening News:*

> **Miss O'Neill said Wardlow picked up an axe and struck her twice on the head with it. She was in bed at the time. Shortly afterwards, he hit her on the head with a can of soup. 'He opened it then and we both had the soup,' she said.**

Crime passionel — or possibly cream of tomato.

I suppose that's one way of making up. But jealousy makes forgiveness and reconciliation awkward. News from the *Evening News:*

> **A Divorce Court judge said today a wife had told him that after confessing to her husband about her adultery with an itinerant ice-cream seller, she wrote a letter to the ice-cream man ending the association. She gave it to her husband, who took it to the man, shook hands with him, and came back with two free sixpenny cornets. This, the wife claimed, meant that her husband had forgiven her.**

The third person who causes problems in a marriage is not always human. Here's a report from the *Evening Standard:*

> **The judge said the dog was her whole life. It was in her bedroom and slept on the bed. If nothing else, it must have been a perfect nuisance if the husband wanted to make love to his wife.**

More evidence from a letter to *Woman's Mirror:*

> **My girl-friend and I were in love and were thinking of getting engaged. Then her father bought her a horse for her birthday and she has not seemed the same since.**

Domestic jealousy need not be a matter of relationships; it sometimes concerns material possessions. Keeping up with the Joneses is the blight of suburban living. Everyone feels they must have things at least as good as their neighbours and preferably better. Certain possessions are deemed to be quite essential. Here's part of a letter written to the *Sunday Pictorial:*

> **Isn't it strange what being a car owner can do for one socially? Until we got ours eighteen months ago, there were quite a few people nearby who never even acknowledged us. Now these people seem to go out of their way to say 'Hello'.**

And of course on that scale of values your car should be bigger and newer than anyone else's. That's supposed to be the way to keep ahead and make sure that it's the neighbours who are jealous of you and not vice versa. Other popular status symbols you need are a few well-chosen ailments and lots of those useless knick-knacks designed for The Man Who Has Everything:

> **If he gets through the day on pills, see that he does it beautifully. Give him a crocodile-skin pill box from Gifts Galore.**

Do You Chew Gum?

Here is a little novelty every one who loves to chew gum will appreciate. "Peggy" is its name. "Peggy" is a convenient and handsomely decorated tin box with a peg in the center to hold your gum when not in use. "Peggy" keeps the gum clean, cool, healthful and handy. "Peggy" can be carried in the pocket, satchel or attached to cord or chain. The more "Peggy" is used the better it is liked. Mailed postpaid on receipt of 5 cents. Agents Wanted. THE PEGGY CO., Dep't D, Cincinnati, O.

And here's another wonderful possession that no one should be without. This one was advertised in *Titbits:*

> **At last! — a warm toilet seat. Like sitting on toast.**

(Let's hope, for everyone's sake, it's not one of those that pops up.)

Failing that, you could buy an electric butter-knife or a navel brush or a pair of solid gold toenail clippers. Then you're sure to be the envy of all your friends.

The whole advertising industry is fuelled by jealousy. It aims to make everyone feel that they are inadequate and that only by buying more than their neighbours can they hope to rise above them. If you can actually do things better than your neighbours, that helps too. Jealousy is a great incentive to make you get on with things. In the words of John Gay:

Envy's a sharper spur than pay.

But though jealousy can spur people on to great heights, there are some people who it's always going to be difficult to beat. What makes for real jealousy is the thought that anyone has an unfair advantage. Many people are jealous of other people's privileges. Let's close with a snippet from the *Daily Sketch:*

Prince Charles, aged 18, passed his driving test first bash yesterday. He went through the 45-minute examination at Isleworth, Middlesex in a special car with a special examiner over a special route. Apart from that it was quite normal.

FEAR

A man was up for his insurance medical. 'Now,' said the doctor, 'just a few more questions. Nothing to be afraid of. Just the medical history. Did your father die a natural death?'

'No,' the man replied, 'he had a doctor.'

During the last war there was a soldier who was terrified of being called up, so he asked a rather bright friend how he could get out of it. 'Easy,' said the friend. 'Do what I did. Buy yourself a truss and say you've been wearing it for years. They'll never call you up.'

So the scared young man did as he was advised. At his army medical examination the officer looked at the truss and asked, 'How long have you been wearing that?'

'Oh, several years.'

'OK,' said the MO, 'I'll put you down for the Camel Corps.'

'What?'

'Oh come on, if you've been wearing a truss upside down for several years, you shouldn't have any trouble riding a camel.'

A little man who was a very proud car-owner was having a drink one day and, when he left the pub, he was furious to see that someone had sprayed his car bright pink. Boiling with rage, he stormed back into the bar and shouted, 'All right. All right. Who painted my car pink?'

From the recess of a corner table an enormous labourer rose to his feet. He was nearly seven foot tall and big with it. 'I did it,' he said.

'Ah. Ah,' the little man stuttered. 'Ah, I've come to tell you the first coat's dry.'

A man went to the psychiatrist. 'Oh, you must help me. I have this horrible recurring nightmare. I see my mother-in-law hunting me with an enormous man-eating alligator. Ooh, it's terrifying... I see these awful yellow, bloodshot eyes, dry scaly skin, these ghastly long sharp teeth... '

The psychiatrist nodded. 'Yes, it does sound pretty nasty.'

'That's nothing,' said the man. 'You wait till I tell you about the alligator.'

An Irish drill sergeant was bawling out a platoon of terrified recruits. 'Look at you,' he yelled. 'Hopeless. Do you call that a straight line? Just fall out and have a look at it.'

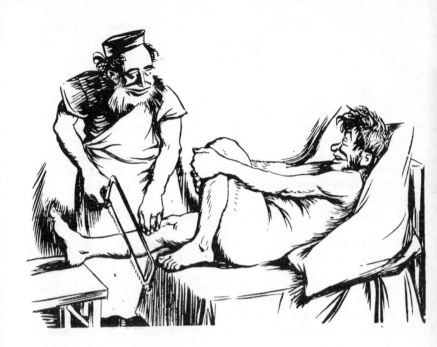

'Doctor, now I'm on the operating table, you can tell me. Is this operation dangerous?'

'That is what we are about to find out.

A little man goes to the psychiatrist. 'It's not about me, it's about my wife. She's a beautiful young woman, but I'm afraid she's going round the bend. She's suddenly developed this phobia. She's terrified someone's trying to steal her clothes.

'Really? What makes you think that?'

'Well, she's even hired a chap to guard them for her. When I got home last night, I found him in the wardrobe.'

Psychologists tell us that we laugh at what we fear. In times of war all kinds of derisory names are invented for the enemy, not because they are funny, but because the reality is so frightening that it needs dressing up to be palatable. But, as well as keeping one's mind off danger, fear is also a useful safety valve to control recklessness. Leonardo da Vinci:

As courage endangers life even so fear preserves it.

Ambrose Bierce:

COWARD, n. One who in a perilous emergency thinks with his feet.

But though fear has the advantage that it sometimes keeps you alive, it also has disadvantages. Edmund Burke.

No passion so effectively robs the mind of all its powers of acting and reasoning as fear.

Bertrand Russell:

Worry is a form of fear, and all forms of fear produce fatigue. A man who has learned not to feel fear will find the fatigue of daily life enormously diminished.

That's easy enough to say, but it's not so easy to follow Russell's advice. We are surrounded by things which inspire fear. Not only the dangers of war, disease, motor accidents and so on, but simple domestic things as well. Here's Dr Johnson on the subject:

Fear is one of the passions of human nature of which it is impossible to divest it. You remember the Emperor Charles V, when he read upon the tombstone of a Spanish nobleman, 'Here lies one who never knew fear!' wittily said, 'Then he never snuffed a candle with his fingers.'

117

He probably never mended a light switch either.

One of the causes of fear which is on the increase is violence in the form of muggings and armed robberies. In the event of attack, it's useful to have some sort of weapon to hand; and sometimes the unlikeliest are the most effective. A news item from the *Daily Mail:*

> **Mrs Mary Garrett, 59, threw a bunch of bananas at a masked bandit with a gun who burst into her shop and post office at Hookwood, near Horley, Surrey yesterday. The man fell down, handed over a toy pistol and said, 'Call the police, I give up.'**

Of course, if the muggers don't get you, there are plenty of natural disasters that can. If you're the sort of person to worry about such things, there are lots out there to worry about. Floods, for instance. Can one be certain that safety precautions are adequate? A report from *The Observer:*

> **London Transport's flood-danger drill is like this: When the standard police warning of an 'exceptional high tide' is received a man is sent to look over the wall at Charing Cross.**

What a comfort that is. A lot of the fears that prey on the mind have a more psychological basis. They aren't real disasters, but irrational anxieties. Sex is the basis of many of them. Fear of women, for example. News from the *Daily Express:*

ZENITH THE ALBINO! (SEE WITHIN.)

THE MOST AMAZING CHARACTER IN MODERN FICTION!

THE UNION JACK LIBRARY

$1\frac{1}{2}$d

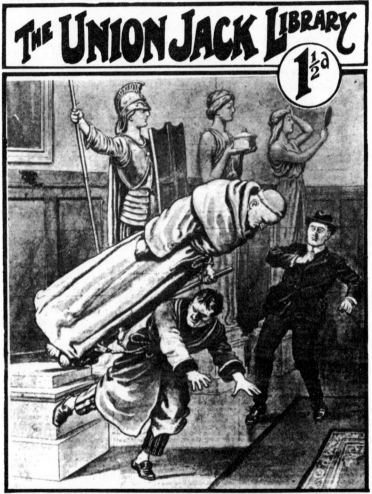

THE CASE OF THE FOUR STATUES

A Remarkable Tale of Mystery & Adventure: Introducing Sexton Blake, Tinker, and Zenith the Albino.

No. 871   EVERY THURSDAY.   June 19th, 1920.

Every time 36-year-old Jack Lee stands by his kitchen window he gets the 'glad eye' from dozens of factory girls. And because he is embarrassed at being their unofficial pin-up boy, the rating valuation of his home has been cut by £3.

Phobias are often related to particular objects or situations. Here's a poem by Hillaire Belloc:

HILDEBRAND,
*Who was frightened by a Passing Motor,
and was brought to Reason.*

'Oh, Murder! What was that, Papa!'
'My child, It was a Motor-Car,
A Most Ingenious Toy!
Designed to Captivate and Charm
Much rather than to rouse Alarm
In any English Boy.

'What would your Great Grandfather who
Was Aide-de-Camp to General Brue,
And lost a leg at... Waterloo,
And... Quatre-Bras and... Ligny too!
And died at Trafalgar! —
What would he have remarked to hear
His Young Descendent shriek with fear,
Because he happened to be near
   A Harmless Motor-Car!
But do not fret about it! Come!
We'll off to Town
   And purchase some!'

Fear of mechanical devices like cars seems to be quite justified. So few of us know anything about the workings of such things to feel much confidence in dealing with them. Electricity is another good example. We all know it works, but not many of us know how, and therefore it's potentially frightening. It certainly disturbed this character described by James Thurber:

Her own mother lived the latter years of her life in the horrible suspicion that electricity was dripping invisibly all over the house.

Oh my goodness there is a mouse !!!

Designed & etched by George Cruikshank

Oh! my good gracious! here is a great
"Black Beadle"!.!! !!!

At least electricity is genuinely dangerous; what makes fear so frustrating as an emotion is that so many of the things one is afraid of are completely unreal. In the words of Shakespeare's Macbeth:

Present fears
Are less than horrible imaginings.

Imagination is responsible for a lot of panics. And the more vivid the imagination, the greater the fear. Montaigne:

He who fears he will suffer, already suffers
because of his fear.

Friedrich Nietzche:

We are terrified by the idea of being terrified.

Mark Twain:

I am an old man and have known a great many troubles,
but most of them never happened.

It's all that business in *Julius Caesar* about cowards dying many times before their deaths, but, though we know it's often irrational, few of us can withstand fear. Particularly in a spooky situation. I mean, say you're alone in an old house. Every rattle of the window becomes a burglar and every creak of the floorboards becomes a ghost. And the idea of ghosts is a pretty scary one, whatever anyone says to the contrary. A letter to *The News of the World*:

May I say a few words that should completely remove fear of ghosts? The information has been given to me by ghosts. If you are privileged to see a ghost do not bolt like a frightened animal; take an intelligent interest in it, talk to it, and ask if you can be of help in any way.

For further information on this spooky subject let's look at a poem by Thomas Hood about body-snatching:

MARY'S GHOST
A Pathetic Ballad

I

'Twas in the middle of the night,
  To sleep young William tried,
When Mary's ghost came stealing in,
  And stood at his bed-side.

II

O William dear! O William dear!
  My rest eternal ceases;
Alas! my everlasting peace
  Is broken into pieces.

III

I thought the last of all my cares
  Would end with my last minute;
But tho' I went to my long home,
  I didn't stay long in it.

IV

The body-snatchers they have come,
  And made a snatch at me;
It's very hard them kind of men
  Won't let a body be!

V

You thought that I was buried deep,
  Quite decent like and chary,
But from her grave in Mary-bone
  They've come and bon'd your Mary.

VI

The arm that used to take your arm
　　Is took to Dr Vyes;
And both my legs are gone to walk
　　The hospital at Guy's.

VII

I vow'd that you should have my hand,
　　But fate gives us denial;
You'll find it there, at Doctor Bell's,
　　In spirits and a phial.

VIII

As for my feet, the little feet
　　You used to call so pretty,
There's one I know, in Bedford Row,
　　The t'other's in the city.

IX

I can't tell where my head is gone,
　　But Doctor Carpue can:
As for my trunk, it's all pack'd up
　　To go by Pickford's van.

X

I wish you'd go to Mr P.
　　And save me such a ride;
I don't half like the outside place,
　　They've took for my inside.

XI

The cock it crows — I must be gone!
　　My William we must part!
But I'll be yours in death, altho'
　　Sir Astley has my heart.

XII

Don't go to weep upon my grave,
　　And think that there I be;
They haven't left an atom there,
　　Of my anatomie.

GHOSTS.

As well as fears of external things, there are many people who are afraid of themselves. This fear is a form of guilt. Samuel Butler:

> **Vouchsafe, O Lord, to keep us this day without being found out.**

Mark Twain:

> **Man is the only animal that blushes. Or needs to.**

Guilt is a fear that there is something wrong with you or what you do. It manifests itself in many ways on many subjects. Money is often a source of guilt. But it shouldn't be, according to the *Weekend Telegraph*:

> **Today a man pretends to be almost ashamed if he inherits a few hundred pounds from his father. This is silly. The instinct for parents to preserve something to pass on to their children is basic even among rodents.**

That sort of information is hardly likely to alleviate a sense of guilt.

Hangovers are a very bad time for guilt feelings, for fear of what you actually said the night before. A small ad from the *Brighton Evening Argus*:

> **Does lady travelling home one night with bottle of sherry and Apocryphal Bible remember long conversation with travelling companion who hereby confesses with shame having advanced blasphemous theories, and has now bitterly repented of them?**

One of the major focuses of guilt is sex. A letter to *The Guardian*:

> **As a mother of three daughters and a pre-school playgroup superintendant, I should like to say how much I agree with Mrs Van Twest about the way in which our fear- and guilt-ridden toy manufacturers shy away from producing male dolls complete with genitalia. My eight-year-old daughter has been indignant on this subject for several years now — and from a very early age used modelling clay to remedy deficiencies.**

Sexual guilt is the basis of the success of the pornography business. People sneak off shamefaced to see smutty films and buy dirty books. But this attitude to the subject is not a modern invention. Here are some extracts from the diary of Samuel Pepys:

> **Jan. 13th, 1668. Stopped at Martin's, my bookseller, where I saw the French book which I did think to have had for my wife to translate, called** *L'escholle des filles*, **but when I come to look in it, it is the most bawdy lewd book that I ever saw... so that I was ashamed of reading it, and so away home.**

> **Feb. 8th. To my bookseller's, and there staid an hour, and bought the idle roughish book,** *L'escholle des filles*; **which I have bought in plain binding, avoiding the buying of it better bound, because I resolve, as soon as I have read it, to burn it, that it may not stand in the list of books, nor among them, to disgrace them if it should be found.**

> **Feb. 9th (Lord's Day). I to my chamber, where I did read through** *L'escholle des filles*, **a lewd book, but what do no wrong once to read for information sake... And after I had done it I burned it, that it might not be among my books to my shame, and so at night to supper and to bed.**

Guilt and fear are unfortunately not just passing emotions. They fester within and cause neuroses. Traumatic experiences can happen to anyone. A report from *The Guardian:*

> **After the hearing Mrs Gamble said she had sent Butch to London to have psychiatric treatment for his inferiority complex. Mr Robert Horsfall, a dog psychiatrist of the Canine Defence League, says he can cure him of his bad habit which springs from an unfortunate experience in early life — he was bitten by a bigger dog!**

Such scarring experiences also happen to people and their lives are never quite the same. Here's a letter that appeared in *Melody Maker:*

> **I travelled around with a group and praised their music and watched their every action. I helped the lead guitarist stick stamps in his album. Then one horrible**

night, as I was walking down a dark alley, the 'boys' set upon me. They held me on the ground, removed every single piece of my clothing and then, grinning lecherously, they stuck 'Ban the Bomb' stickers and World Cup stamps all over me. It was horrid. I can never now live a happily married life, because every time I see my husband's priceless collection (he's got several penny reds and a jubilee issue) I just pass clean out. So please, rampant group members, control yourselves.

I wonder if there's a word for that particular condition. I suppose it should be philatephobia, but I should think it's pretty rare.

So what advice can I give on the avoidance of fear, as I end this chapter? I can only say live your life as safely as you can. And, if you see a warning notice, like this one on a pylon, obey it:

BEWARE!

TO TOUCH THESE WIRES IS INSTANT DEATH

Anyone found doing so will be prosecuted

LUST

Mum said if I look at pictures like this
I'll turn into stone.... I've started !

I had a job once at the YMCA Maintenance. Had to check the central heating was working in all the girls' bedrooms. Seven quid a week. Not much, I know, but it was all I could afford.

The bride and groom were finally alone. 'May I kiss you, darling?' he asked.

'Oh God,' she said. 'Another amateur.'

During the Middle Ages two beautiful young maidens and their ugly old nurse were cowering in an upstairs room while barbarians laid siege to their castle. Eventually the enemy broke in and ran about screaming with delight, looting and pillaging. A group of them burst down the door of the girls' room and stood looking at them lasciviously. It was the moment for a noble action. The elder girl stepped forward. 'Do what you like to me and my sister,' she said, 'but we beg you not to touch our aged nurse.'

'Shut up,' said the nurse. 'War is war.'

An interviewer was going round an old people's home talking to the inmates. He went up to one very old gentleman. 'And may I ask how old you are, sir?'

'Ninety-seven.'

'And to what do you attribute your great age, sir?'

'I've never smoked, never drunk and never had anything to do with women.'

He moved on to another even older-looking man. 'And how old are you, sir?'

'One hundred and one years old.'

'And to what do you attribute your great age?'

'Never had nothing to do with women.'

At last he went up to a man who looked even older than all the others. He was bent, wizened and toothless. 'Tell me, sir,' asked the interviewer, 'what's kept you going so long?'

'Lust,' croaked the shrivelled figure. 'Lust. Women. Lust. Yes, lots and lots of women.'

'And how old are you?'

'Twenty-three next birthday.'

A vicar was preaching a sermon on the Ten Commandments. When he came to 'Thou Shalt Not Steal', he noticed that a meek-looking man in the front row suddenly looked very anxious and uncomfortable. The vicar continued and, when he came to 'Thou Shalt Not Commit Adultery', the man in the front row suddenly looked very relieved.

After the service the vicar was curious and asked the man about his strange reactions. 'Well, you see,' came the reply, 'when you said "Thou Shalt Not Steal", I thought someone had stolen my umbrella, but when you got to "Thou Shalt Not Commit Adultery", I remembered where I had left it.'

'Do you know, I'd only been in hospital a week when complications set in.'
  'Why? What happened?'
  'The day nurse caught me kissing the night nurse.'

Boy to girlfriend — 'I dreamt about you last night.'
  Girlfriend — 'Did you?'
  Boy — 'No, you wouldn't let me.'

Lust is one of the Seven Deadly Sins and also part of one of the world's greatest pleasures. As a result, attitudes to it are always a bit ambivalent and perhaps this is why it features so universally in humour. Stories of lust and its attempted gratification are part of comedy in all fields — from the sophistication of Restoration Comedy to the bawdiness of dirty jokes. I suppose the reason is that lust does occupy a disproportionate amount of people's thinking time. Malcolm Muggeridge:

It has to be admitted that we English have sex on the brain, which is a very unfortunate place to have it.

Anything you've got on the brain tends to take up rather a lot of your time. Here's a remark by Mrs Alfred Kinsey, wife of the famous researcher into sexual matters:

I don't see so much of Alfred any more since he got so interested in sex.

Perhaps we should now have a quick definition, just to clarify our terms of reference. From Clifford Odets:

SEX — **The poor man's polo.**

Blame for all kinds of troubles has been laid at the door of lust. Robert Burton, from his *Anatomy of Melancholy:*

Thunder and lightning, wars, fires, plagues, have not done that mischief to mankind as this burning lust.

But existence would be pretty dull without it. Dr Johnson on the subject:

Some desire is necessary to keep life in motion.

Mrs Draper taking unwarrantable Liberties with
William Pinfold. —— See Trials for Adultery, N.º 10, Page 20.
4.th Novr 1780, by S. Bladen.

According to tradition, lust is strongest in young people. I'm not sure that that's true; it may just be that as people grow older, they accept it more and don't spend so much time talking about it. (Come to think of it, I'm not sure that that's true either.) But it is certainly true that for the young, the facts of life are new and exciting. A report from the *Sunday Express*:

Edinburgh's Director of Education, referring to sex education, is reported to have said, 'Teachers noticed a new look in children's eyes after an experimental course.'

Actually it's quite an old look. But some kids just seem to know the facts without being taught. A letter from the *Daily Mirror:*

Why all this fuss about sex education in schools? I am sixteen and I taught my mother about reproduction, using the correct biological terms. The present generation of parents cannot tell their children how they came to be born because they do not know.

"Mildred Willmott . . . Doris Wormold . . . Alice . . ."

Young people have always been prepared to find things out for themselves; it's just natural curiosity. Here's Mary Quant, telling her experiences to the *Sunday Mirror:*

> **He never washed up anything, so the kitchen was awful. He used every plate, every piece of cutlery in the house, and these just remained stacked up by the sink, week after week. To me, this way of life was distinctly bohemian and exciting. It was the right background for our first experiments in sex.**

It is supposed to be the parents' duty to keep a watchful eye over the morals of their offspring, and to keep a balance between restraint and freedom. A difficult task, as this report from the *Birmingham Post* reveals:

> **The mother complained that her son, an only child, was becoming truculent, had started smoking, had been seen entering a public house and was keeping company with a girl. Inspector McCann began to investigate. 'I found that the son was 36,' he stated.**

Anxiety over people's sexual behaviour can often develop into prudery, which is more often a comment on the person shocked than on what they find shocking. The Victorians were very strict on all matters of decorum. Here's an extract from a book of etiquette by Lady Gough, published in 1863:

> **The perfect hostess will see to it that the works of male and female authors be properly separated on her bookshelves. Their proximity, unless they happen to be married, should not be tolerated.**

It takes a really suspicious mind to be that devious. But prudes on the whole are suspicious. Maria Edgeworth, writing in 1814:

> **I hate scandal — at least I am not so fond of it as the lady of whom it was said she could not see the poker and tongs standing together without suspecting something wrong!**

Prudery takes various forms. Some people believe that what is sauce for the gander in these matters should be kept well clear of the goose. A report from the *News Chronicle:*

> **A dapper, white-bearded Cambridge professor told yesterday how he went to the local authority for sex education pamphlets for his two sons. 'But I was so alarmed in case my wife should see them that I had to throw them out.'**

If you disapprove of sex, you can just pretend it doesn't exist and hope it'll go away. (It won't, incidentally.) From *Our Church Review:*

> **At both services in the morning it is intended to preach a series of sermons on the 'Deadly Sins', omitting lust.**

And, if lust remains in spite of being ignored, perhaps a system of rationing should be brought in. This was recommended by Andrew Borde in about 1542 in his *Compendyous Regyment or a Dyetary of Health:*

> **Beware of veneryous acts before the first sleep, and specially beware of such things after dinner or after a full stomach, for it doth ingender the cramp and the gout and other displeasures.**

Borde also reckoned he had a cure for lust, which would take the sufferer's mind off it completely. I think it might well work, because all you have to do is:

To leap into a great vessel of cold water, or to put nettles in the codpiece.

'When you've seen one you've seen them all.'

Some individuals have got so depressed by lust that they have criticised the system, wishing that the whole sexual function could be changed. Here are Martin Luther's alternative suggestions:

The reproduction of mankind is a great marvel and mystery. Had God consulted me in the matter, I should have advised him to continue the generation of the species by fashioning them of clay.

Unfortunately for Luther, God never did consult him in the matter. Sir Thomas Browne also put forward an interesting suggestion in the seventeenth century:

> I could wish that we might procreate like trees, without conjunction; or that there were any way to perpetuate the world without this trivial and vulgar way of coition; it is the foolishest act a wise man commits in his whole life, nor is there anything that will deject his cold imagination more, when he shall consider what an odde and unworthy piece of folly he hath committed. I speak not in prejudice, nor am adverse from that sweet sex, but naturally amorous of all that is beautiful; I can looke a whole day with delight upon a handsome picture, though it be but of a horse.

Well, I suppose everyone's entitled to an opinion.

Most of us can, fortunately, reconcile ourselves to the existence of lust. Its only disadvantage is that it can be a distraction. News from the *Daily Mail:*

> When I first glimpse the backs of women's knees I seem to hear the first movement of Beethoven's Pastoral Symphony.

Well, it takes all sorts. Here's an anonymous eighteenth-century poem:

> We're a' dry wi' the drinkin' o't
> We're a' dry wi' the drinkin' o't,
> The minister kissed the fiddler's wife,
> And couldna preach for thinkin' o't.

Lust does make concentration difficult, but a lot of people are prepared to spend money on stimulating it to make concentration even more difficult. Here's a report from the *Oxford Times:*

> 'Samantha' stripped down to her G-string and when she ran off there were boos from the audience because she had not stripped naked. On July 8th when he again went to the club with another officer, P. C. May said he was asked by the doorman, 'Are you one of the boys from Balliol?

Another from the *Daily Mirror:*

> Mr Joseph Mouratt, owner of the Gallipoli Restaurant in Bishopsgate, City, explained: 'I have discovered that City gentlemen with their wives have different views about how near a belly dancer may dance. I have instructed the eleven dancers — five men and six women — how to behave. If there is a titled dignitary in the room they dance only on the stage.' Mr Mouratt added: 'If there are City Sheriffs, Aldermen or councillors they may dance within four feet. Bankers may be approached at two feet and insurance executives at one foot.'

What's so special about insurance executives?

The trouble with lust is that, though there's nothing wrong with it in itself, it can lead to immorality. Not always, though, as this misprint from the *Liverpool Echo* shows:

> Going overseas? Emigration, business or lust pleasure. Immediate passages available.

And here's the other side of lust in a misprint from the *Daily Telegraph:*

> The Manx Government plans to relax regulations on boarding houses to make more beds available for tourist sin late August and September.

Sin. That's where lust can lead. Particularly when the sun comes out. Lord Byron:

> What men call gallantry, and gods adultery,
> Is much more common where the climate's sultry.

Adultery is still one of the most important causes of divorce. Mind you, things do change. Here's a report from a wartime *Reynolds News:*

> **West End Solicitors, who before the war netted five-figure incomes from divorce cases, have been heavily hit by the blackout. In the winter months, at any rate, private inquiry agents are helpless. Adultery cannot be proved because identification is impossible in the pitch dark.**

Sometimes one feels the whole business of lust must have been simpler in less sophisticated times. An unintentional comment due to misspelling in a schoolboy's examination answer:

> **The early Britons made their houses of mud and there was rough mating on the floors.**

Or perhaps, in sexual matters, as in everything else, one does better by concentrating on practical considerations. A small ad from the *Lincolnshire Chronicle:*